AMERICA
LOST AND FOUND

The key to Americas's **FUTURE**
may well lie in her **PAST**

RICHARD PHILIP AVILA

SILVERSMITH
PRESS

Published by Silversmith Press—Houston, Texas
www.silversmithpress.com

Copyright © 2024 Richard Philip Avila

All rights reserved.

This book, or parts thereof, may not be reproduced in any form or by any means without written permission from the author, except for brief passages for purposes of reviews. For more information, contact the publisher at office@publishandgo.com.

The views and opinions expressed herein belong to the author and do not necessarily represent those of the publisher.

ISBN 978-1-961093-66-9 (Softcover Book)
ISBN 978-1-961093-67-6 (eBook)

This book is first dedicated to the Lord Jesus Christ who, by His Spirit, directed and inspired me to complete this writing assignment. I also wish to dedicate it to my wonderful wife, Judy Avila, who encouraged me throughout the process and served as one of my first readers. Heartfelt thanks go out to my pastor and dear friend, Greg Simas; to my beloved son Jared Avila; and my cherished friends John and Mary Starr, who all served as my first readers, providing invaluable insight and in-depth feedback, which I applied often in my initial editing. Finally, I want to acknowledge and thank Joanna Hunt who served as my writing coach. She kept me on task and focused on the major things. I am very thankful for all your input and love you all immensely.

CONTENTS

Introduction vii

Chapter 1: So Where Are We as a Nation? 1
Chapter 2: "Never Discuss Religion or Politics" 14
Chapter 3: "Mommy, Did I Really Come from a Monkey?" 25
Chapter 4: Whose Body Is It? 40
Chapter 5: Of the Children 49
Chapter 6: Gender Conditioning
Chapter 7: The Fathers Knew Best 89
Chapter 8: Embracing the Fear of the Lord 101
Chapter 9: Not of This World—Part 1 108
Chapter 10: Not of This World—Part 2 125
Chapter 11: And Another Thing 143

Resources 149
End Notes 151

INTRODUCTION

Finally, my brethren, be strong in the Lord and in the power of His might. Put on the whole armor of God, so that you may be able to stand against the wiles of the devil. For we do not wrestle against flesh and blood, but against principalities, against powers, against the rulers of the darkness of this age, against spiritual hosts of wickedness in the heavenly places. Therefore, take up the whole armor of God, that you may be able to withstand in the evil day, and having done all to stand. Stand, therefore (Ephesians 6:10-14).

When Paul wrote this epistle to the believers in Ephesus, they lived under the iron-fisted rule of the Roman Empire. They did not enjoy the benefits of a free society as we do in America. Therefore, if Roman law required them to violate their faith and practices in Christ, they would have to stand for their beliefs in direct defiance of Rome. The cost for such defiance was great indeed, and many paid the ultimate price.

Fast forward to today. Although many governmental bodies in the US have grown increasingly hostile to biblical beliefs, practices, and specifically Christianity, we still enjoy unparalleled freedom to express and practice our beliefs.

According to Wikipedia:

> Christianity is the most prevalent religion in the United States. Estimates from 2021 suggest that of the entire U.S. population (332 million) about 63% is Christian (210 million). The majority of Christian Americans are Protestant Christians (140 million; 42%), though there are also significant numbers of American Roman Catholics (70 million; 21%)[1]

Given that nearly two-thirds of Americans profess to be believers in Jesus Christ and therefore would hold to the veracity of the Bible to direct their religious beliefs and social conduct, how is it, then, that the predominant cultural influence in America is secular, humanist, and to a significant degree, atheistic?

There are, I believe, two overarching reasons why the societal influence of Christians and Christianity in general has greatly diminished in the last century. You could probably think of several others as well. The first would be the voting habits, or the lack thereof, amongst Christians. Consider the voting habits among Christians and Catholics in the following article from the *Christian Post* citing *Pew Research*:

> The share of registered voters in the United States who say they are Christian has declined by about 15% since

INTRODUCTION

2008 while the number of religiously unaffiliated voters has nearly doubled, Pew Research Center data suggests.

Pew drew the data from a balanced survey of over 360,000 registered voters surveyed over a 25-year span that include over 12,000 voters questioned in 2018 and 2019. The data indicates that 64% of all registered voters surveyed in 2019 self-identified as Christian. That figure is down from 79% of registered voters surveyed in 2008 who identified themselves as followers of Christ. The study shows that the decline in registered Christian voters is most stark in the Democratic Party.[2]

Over the last several years it has been a well-established trend that fewer and fewer Christians vote. They either feel that involvement in human government is unspiritual or are simply apathetic to the process. I wonder how those early Roman Christians would have responded to being given the right to vote for their leaders. Given the fact that thousands of their brethren had been barbarically martyred at the hands of the Romans, I'm fairly confident that they would have praised God ecstatically for this incredible blessing and would have flocked to the polls to vote for godly leaders.

But in modern America, there is a disconnect for many Christians regarding this fundamental duty. Many professed Christians vehemently express disgust with the godless legislation that pours out from local, state, and federal governing bodies. Yet many of these same believers do not support or vote for the best possible candidates!

Shouldn't we as Christians, if we do not like the election outcomes, take a look in the mirror to discover why so many "rascals" have managed to get themselves into public office? Could our absence at the polls be part of the explanation? I think yes.

Secondly, a significant number of professed Christians are either uninformed about biblical truths relating to social conduct or consider certain of those truths not to be relevant by today's societal norms. This second reason is in some ways more troubling than the first. It appears that many Christians do not truly embrace the Bible as the actual Word of God. They see it as being somewhat antiquated and not fully applicable to a modern "progressive" society. It seems many of us have forgotten that "The Ten Commandments" are not The Ten Suggestions.

I'm sure you'd agree that any born-again believer in Christ must be awake to the present realities in our culture. Before I was born again in Christ, I was a card-carrying member of the kingdom of darkness, well-practiced in all its ways. When I became a Christian in 1979 and began a serious walk with the Lord in 1980, I didn't need anyone to point out to me the difference between living in darkness—which I'd just been delivered from—and living in the light of being a new creation in Christ. But what was a black-and-white distinction for me now seems to be lost on many who claim to follow Christ.

In 2016, prior to the general elections, I sent out an email to all the Christians whose email addresses I had to provide them with information and even evidence from the

INTRODUCTION

Democrat-published platform of the utterly ungodly policy stances and beliefs they were propagating. To my shock, I received responses from people who were offended that I would use their contact information to disseminate "political information." Some replied saying that they just held a different "perspective." A dear friend of mine relayed a similar account when having asked a couple of his friends how they reconciled voting for candidates who ardently supported abortion on demand, the LGBTQ agenda, and other ungodly policies with their Christian faith. They indicated that their agreement with other "social issues" the candidates endorsed was more important to them than any one single issue such as abortion. To me, this was a rude awakening to find out that many who claim to be followers of Christ would turn a blind eye to views and practices that blatantly violated the Word of God.

Whether this ambiguity is due to a lack of biblical understanding or a buckling to immense societal pressures in America, it indicates that we as Christians are not unified in commitment to our stated belief of being followers of Jesus Christ. Today many voices bemoan the fact that, as a nation, we are not unified. Many Christians share this concern to the point of trying to find common ground with those who are outside the family of God. Some hold that America could be unified in belief and lifestyle if Christians would just compromise a little on biblical commands and standards. But the truth is the divide between the citizens in America is not between black vs. white, rich vs. poor, or male vs. female. These are artificial divisions as a result of the fallen state of all humanity. No, the real division has always been and always will be between those who believe and follow God and those who do not.

Listen to what Jesus said on the issue of unity:

> Do not think that I came to bring peace on earth. I did not come to bring peace but a sword. For I have come to "set a man against his father, a daughter against her mother, and a daughter-in-law against her mother-in-law"; and "a man's enemies will be those of his own household" (Matthew 10:34).

Paul too, writing to the Corinthians, forbids fellowship between people of light with those of darkness: "Do not be unequally yoked together with unbelievers. For what fellowship has righteousness with lawlessness? And what communion has light with darkness" (2 Corinthians 6:14)?

We need to have it settled in our hearts and minds that unity among all people is only possible through the cross and the cleansing blood of Jesus Christ. The only question remaining is who is going to influence the nation, the godly or the ungodly?

The purpose of this book is not to point out and highlight our shortcomings as Christians. The purpose is to be a help to all who are or wish to be sincere followers of Jesus so that we know God's Word, His heart, and His expectations for us, His children. Just as the apostle James states in his epistle, the outward profession of faith without a tangible and visible outworking of that faith is self-deception

INTRODUCTION

at best. At worst, it is a refusal to walk in obedience to the Word. Jesus Himself said, "Why do you call me 'Lord, Lord' and do not do the things I say" (Luke 6:64).

I believe that most Christians desire to demonstrate their faith in everyday life. But, like me, they tend to lack boldness and confidence in communicating their faith. Would you agree with the observation that America has been increasingly doing a one-eighty from being "One nation under God" to a nation that seems bent on extricating itself from any reference of and responsibility to the Almighty?

In the first several chapters of this book, we will explore the current state of our American culture and how far it has drifted from those who shed their blood to establish this wonderful nation. The concluding chapters will endeavor to inspire you on how you can take some basic steps to be a more active and visible ambassador for Christ—in other words, how to be "salt and light."

Delving into the depths of darkness that now marks "America the Beautiful" can be an overwhelming exercise, but don't be discouraged. The first step in defeating any enemy is to know where his strongholds are and the strength of his forces. Do be encouraged as the Lord has given us "great and precious promises" that we will be victorious in this battle for our God-ordained country, America.

Yet in all these things we are more than conquerors through Him who loved us (Romans 8:37).

Behold, I give you the authority to trample on serpents and scorpions, and over all the power of the enemy, and nothing shall by any means hurt you (Luke 10:9).

And the God of peace will crush Satan under your feet shortly (Romans 16:20).

CHAPTER 1
SO WHERE ARE WE AS A NATION?

But know this, that in the last days perilous times will come: For men will be lovers of themselves, lovers of money, boasters, proud, blasphemers, disobedient to parents, unthankful, unholy unloving, unforgiving, slanderers, without self-control, brutal, despisers of good, traitors, headstrong, haughty, lovers of pleasure rather than lovers of God, having a form of godliness but denying its power. And from such people turn away! (2 Timothy 3:1-5)

I first read this scripture when I was a young believer and thought, "Wow, that sounds awful! I'm glad things aren't that bad now!" I knew a lot of things had gone awry in our country, but in the afterglow of the "Jesus People Movement," there were lots of new churches springing up, supernatural healing was happening, and a newfound expression of spiritual gifts was on the upswing. Through the mid-1980s people were still coming to the Lord in significant numbers.

Unfortunately, during this period there was also a strong sentiment permeating the Body of Christ that the Lord's return was imminent. I don't know about you, but for me, this gave rise to the mindset that I didn't need to be concerned about planning for the future but rather focus solely on bringing people to Jesus. Don't get me wrong. I still believe that leading people to Jesus should always be our primary ministry focus, but I have come to realize that it is not to be our only one. The Lord will return, but I believe that it will not be as soon as we had imagined.

THE BATTLE IS OVER WHEN THE ENEMY CONCEDES

By the beginning of 1945, during World War II, the German and the Japanese defeats were a foregone conclusion, even before the formal surrenders occurred. But until the German and Japanese surrenders were formalized, the Allied forces couldn't relax assuming the position of the victors. Any easing of the battle would have prolonged the war, cost more lives, and delayed victory.

Is this not the same situation we are in as the church of Jesus? We know that ultimate victory is assured; in fact, the victory has already been won, but we must continue to fight and engage the enemy until the actual return of Jesus. Doesn't it seem that in this war of culture in America that we Christians have largely stopped fighting, choosing rather to just hunker down until the second coming? Other Christians appear to have chosen the appeasement route with the enemy. Continuing the World War II analogy,

CHAPTER 1: SO WHERE ARE WE AS A NATION?

Great Britain under Prime Minister Neville Chamberlain pursued appeasement when first confronted with the rise of Nazi Germany with his famous slogan "Peace for our time." Less than a year later, the Germans invaded Poland and World War II broke out. In our case, appeasement manifests as: affirming abortion in certain circumstances, sporting "Pride" flags on church monument signs, being silent about startling changes in public school curriculums, and in general aligning our beliefs and practices with those operating in direct opposition to the Word of God. Now hear me in this. Agreeing with and even endorsing the enemy in a time of war is known as "treason." It is time that the gauntlet thrown down by Joshua to the Israelites is thrown down to the Body of Christ. It's time to take sides—*Choose for yourselves this day whom you will serve . . . but as for me and my house, we will serve the Lord* (Joshua 24:15).

REVERSE METAMORPHOSIS?

The metamorphosis of a caterpillar is from a more limited and basic creature into a brilliantly colored, intricately designed flying machine known as a butterfly, now able to participate in the pollination of a variety of flowers, allowing them to reproduce. What a picture of the potential that God places within each of us, His creations. The same can be seen in the development of nations. Although far from perfect, the advent of Christianity brought the nations of Europe and Scandinavia, especially, to a metamorphosis

AMERICA: LOST AND FOUND

from primarily savage and barbaric pagan tribes into highly civilized nations.

In the last hundred-plus years, however, the beliefs and values of these same Western nations, specifically, the United States of America, have morphed significantly in the opposite direction. Does it seem to you, as it does to me, that things really may be as bad as described in 2 Timothy now? As late as the 1950s into the early 1960s, America embraced traditional Judeo-Christian values. Beliefs and practices regarding truthfulness, honesty, personal responsibility, hard work, and respect for our fellow human beings were common societal norms. These ideals were accompanied by a basic belief in the God of the Bible to whom we must all give an account of how we lived our lives.

Attorney John Whitehead described the biblical worldview as foundational to the law of any civilized society and applied it specifically to the writing of the Constitution.

> The first type of law is the fundamental law upon which the culture and society are established. . . . the laws of nature and of nature's God. The higher law is clearly expressed in God's revelation as ultimately found in the Bible. In this, the higher law has its sustenance.
> The second type of law, Constitutional law, provides the form of civil government to protect the God-given rights of the people. The people can base their institutions upon Constitutional law, in conjunction with the higher or fundamental law. . . .[1]

CHAPTER 1: SO WHERE ARE WE AS A NATION?

> The bottom line is that man's laws must have its origin in God's revelation. Any law that contradicts biblical revelation is illegitimate. . . . After all, it is the Creator who endows man with rights, which the law is to protect. Succinctly put, there is a law, a system of absolutes, derived from biblical principles that transcends man and his institutions. It existed before man and will exist after him.[2]

TRUTHFULNESS

Fast forward to today (2024) and we see that the landscape of ideas and values is vastly different than those generally embraced throughout the history of our country. To cite an example, a study from Currents, a University of Wisconsin-La Crosse blog, find that: "75% of the people surveyed over a 91 consecutive day period reported telling at least two lies per day."[3]

Such decisions on practicing truthfulness, as an example, are often based on the notion that it may be better to be less than truthful with another person if we deem that telling them the actual truth may cause them pain. This also touches on honoring others, in that lying to someone, even when you judge your motives to be sincere, is actually dishonoring them. The truth is, when we lie to someone, we are choosing the path of least resistance, not wishing to engage in the uncomfortable discussion that may ensue. We have sacrificed "speaking the truth in love" to the other person, thereby denying them the right to know the reality of a situation in preference for our own desire to avoid discomfort. This practice is really nothing more than basic selfishness. And in case you think that I am just pointing the proverbial finger at everyone else at large, I confess being "guilty as charged" numerous times in my life. But as the scripture says "the truth will set you (and others) free."

HONESTY

And it doesn't stop at lying. In an article by Chris Kolmar of Zippia, the Career Expert reports that 75% of employees admit to stealing from their employer at least once. Employee theft accounts for employer losses of $50 billion a year.[4]

It has become very easy to take something that doesn't belong to you if you can conjure up a plausible justification for your actions. "Well, that $20 bill was just sitting by the coffee machine in the break room. Finder's keepers," you might say to yourself as you pocket the newly discovered treasure. What might your response have been toward the person who took the $20 if you had been the one who had accidentally left it there and came back hoping to retrieve it? How about, "I work like a slave for my company; if I want to take home a few pens from the office, there is nothing wrong with that—I've earned them." Or, "You know there have been a lot of occasions that I've worked over a few minutes and never added any extra time to my time card. So what's wrong with adding a few hours now and again to make up for it? I'm sure it will all even out."

CHAPTER 1: SO WHERE ARE WE AS A NATION?

PERSONAL RESPONSIBILITY

I'm sure you know the old blues song "No One Knows the Trouble I've Seen." There is no doubt that the troubles we encounter in life are real, and that many people have had extraordinarily severe levels of trouble, cannot be denied. However, a major value historically in America has been the commitment to face troubles head-on and tackle all obstacles that arise.

Taking personal responsibility for one's situation and actions was a given. Our current culture has drifted into an unfortunate practice that I term "excusism." In the past, embracing a plethora of excuses (excusism) for why you couldn't progress, succeed, or accomplish anything significant in life was seen as a weakness of character, something to be avoided, not embraced. But now with secularist ideologies which put forth ideas such as "We are solely products of our environment" we are encouraged to negate taking personal responsibility for our lives. We say, "It's not my fault I am the way I am: it's where I was born; it's my parent's fault; it's because my family was poor; my third-grade teacher didn't like me; I was made fun of and bullied by my classmates; and ..." you fill in the blanks. Truthfully, many have endured far more severe life challenges than those previously mentioned. Don't get me wrong, I'm not trying to diminish the seriousness of how things that have happened to us can affect our wellbeing. I'm merely pointing out that, culturally, how we respond to the issues of life has dramatically shifted in the last sixty or so years.

AMERICA: LOST AND FOUND

History is replete with wonderful stories of how some of the greatest men and women who have ever lived overcame horrendous obstacles and rose to tremendous heights. Among them are such towering figures as Benjamin Franklin, Abraham Lincoln, Winston Churchill, and Harriet Tubman. These are but a few of the giants in history who exercised the courage to overcome the hand they were dealt and pressed on to fulfill their destinies, and we are all the better for it.

I often think about the significance of the story of one George Bailey, a fictional character from the classic movie *It's a Wonderful Life*. If you haven't watched this film, I strongly encourage you to see it. George Bailey is given the divine opportunity to see what the world would have been like if he had never been born. So as not to ruin the story if you haven't seen the film, suffice it to say that the lives of many people would have been greatly diminished had George Bailey never been born. It is a powerful example of one man taking personal responsibility for the issues of life that he faced, often at the expense of his own dreams and desires. And the blessings that resulted in positively affecting an entire community and beyond. We, like George, can always choose our own interests and desires above those around us. In the end, George finds himself in a place of joy and contentment, and makes no excuse for the paths he has chosen. Excusism is a road that leads a person to unrealized dreams and unfulfilled potential. The result will be a diminishing not only of our own lives but also of the lives of the many family members and friends that surround us.

CHAPTER 1: SO WHERE ARE WE AS A NATION?

ENTERPRISE AND HARD WORK

The Puritan Work Ethic is a long-standing value system rooted in the tenet that all of one's activities in life ought to be done as unto the Lord. In other words, everyday tasks and duties should be done honestly, diligently, and to the best of one's ability, for we do not know which day will be our last. The Puritans did not believe in delaying or procrastinating doing what was right when it was in their power to do so in the present. This Puritan work ethic, which has been adhered to by Christians and non-Christians alike, has been the driving force instrumental in America's success. Nations where Christian ethics have been the most influential are marked with great success: sociologically, economically, and morally. In contrast, and this ties in closely with personal responsibility, today's cultural attitudes to work reflect an entitlement mentality overriding the belief in earning what you receive. The idea that one should be given everything one needs and desires simply because one exists robs the individual of the self-esteem that results from utilizing their gifts and abilities to accomplish successes in life. This also harms society as a whole in that resources that rightly belong to others, by virtue of their hard work, are taken away in the form of increased taxation and given to those deemed entitled to these resources.

I do believe that a compassionate society will make provision for those who truly cannot provide for themselves, as in the case of physically or mentally disabled persons. However, as we saw during the COVID-19 crisis in 2020, there were a large number of people who would not work for their living in lieu of the fact that they could receive more money from the government by just staying home. This is a tremendous cultural shift when as recent as the 1960s it was still considered shameful to take government handouts when a person was able to work to provide for themselves and their family.

The ethic of working hard to support one's self and family was wonderfully illustrated in a scene from the movie *The Legend of Bagger Vance*. A dialogue occurs between the amateur golfer Judah played by Matt Damon, one of my favorite actors, and a young boy who is carefully following this historic golf tournament. In one scene the boy expresses his embarrassment over his previously successful father working as a street sweeper during the Great Depression, which he considered undignified, especially when some of the other boys' fathers were accepting government subsidies, and thus "maintaining their dignity." Judah sternly responds that the boy's father was doing what was honorable, willing to work to support his family while others were content to sit at home and collect "free money" from the government. Martin Luther King Jr. described hard and honorable work this way:

> If it falls to your lot to be a street sweeper, sweep streets like Michelangelo painted pictures, sweep streets like Beethoven composed music ... Sweep streets like Shakespeare wrote poetry. Sweep streets so well that all the

CHAPTER 1: SO WHERE ARE WE AS A NATION?

host of heaven and earth will have to pause and say: Here lived a great street sweeper who swept his job well.[5]

This ethical shift from doing whatever was necessary to provide for oneself and family to being content in taking government handouts, as stated earlier, only serves to denigrate the value and potential of the individual and deprive society as a whole of the personal contribution that each person can bring to that society.

RESPECT FOR OTHERS

One need only take a short drive on America's roadways to experience firsthand how common courtesy and respect for others has deteriorated. I'm always amazed at how the desire to "be first" often supersedes the desire to extend consideration to other drivers. The other day I was driving on the freeway. The traffic conditions were heavy. I needed to change lanes to the right to make my exit. When a large enough space presented itself, I put on my turn signal to notify the drivers behind me of my intention to change lanes. Immediately the driver behind me in the lane I was attempting to change into began to speed up and prevent me from changing lanes. Again, the traffic was heavy, and there was nothing to be gained by this driver's action, but they thought it a better decision to cut me off rather than allow me to change lanes and make my exit.

There is an appropriate line from the movie *Ghost Town* that calls out this type of self-centered action. It says, and I'll change out the expletives, "One day you're going to look in the mirror and ask yourself, what did I really get out of being such a bleeping jerk?" Although selfish behavior has always been a negative characteristic of mankind throughout history, the Christian ethic commanded by Jesus, "Do unto others as you would have them do unto you" is often abandoned in our "modern" society. Certainly, there are still many people who put others first in their daily interactions, but common courtesy and consideration for others before oneself is no longer an overarching societal norm as it once was in America.

The shifting values from an otherly-focused society to one that is far more self-focused has not served us well. An ever-increasing number of decisions are based on lawlessness, greed, and self-interest; legislatively we have been forced to open a virtual Pandora's Box of new laws and the resulting waterfall of trivial lawsuits. All because we essentially refuse to behave ourselves and extend preference to others.

So where are we now as a culture? It seems we have come to the place where it can be said of us as a nation, "Oh, how the mighty have fallen."

When I was a child, in the late 1950s to the early 1960s, the ideal that "a man's word was his bond" still resonated with many people. This ideal was reinforced by many of the movies and television shows of that era like *Leave It to Beaver* and *Father Knows Best*. These TV shows usually closed by imparting some lesson in good morals or proverbial wisdom. However, the messaging of contemporary

CHAPTER 1: SO WHERE ARE WE AS A NATION?

television sitcoms is a huge departure from the type of wholesome programming that marked TV shows in the past. The days when the value of doing the right thing, regardless of what the personal cost may be, may seem a distant image in the rearview mirror of what is accepted and practiced in our nation today.

I loved one of the lines from the movie *Cool Hand Luke*, starring Paul Newman as Luke. Luke was incarcerated in a southern labor camp for destroying parking meters while in a drunken stupor. At the time he was serving his sentence, his mother passed away. The warden's policy was to lock up any prisoner whose mother had died, in the "box," an outhouse-sized structure where prisoners were confined for violating camp rules. According to the warden, this was because men start thinking about wanting to escape to be at "momma's" funeral. As the guards put Luke into "the box," one of them says to him, "Sorry, Luke, just doin' my job," to which Luke profoundly replies, "Callin' it your job don't make it right."

CHAPTER 2
"NEVER DISCUSS RELIGION OR POLITICS"

This adage has continually been put forth and widely accepted as a means to avoid heated arguments, particularly among family and friends. If ever the enemy of our souls has been more successful at promoting his narrative, convincing followers of Christ to just shut up and to be nice to everyone certainly tops the list.

DISCUSS JESUS, NOT RELIGION

The truth is knowing Jesus is not about religion; it's a personal relationship. Your testimony, relating your personal experience and encounter with Jesus, is not only powerful evidence of the reality of God but that He affords us the opportunity not only to know Him but also to have a personal relationship with Him. Besides, people like to hear the personal experiences of others. Everyone loves a good story. You don't have to necessarily preach either.

CHAPTER 2: "NEVER DISCUSS RELIGION OR POLITICS"

Tell the story well and you'll likely have the opportunity to communicate the love of God that He demonstrated through Jesus.

Resist being drawn into religious arguments, and always circle back to the "Good News." "Remind them of these things, charging them before the Lord not to strive about words to no profit, to the ruin of the hearers" (2 Timothy 2:14). This scripture is directed to believers, yet the same principle holds true when talking with those who have not yet believed. Bear in mind that "The natural man does not receive the things of the spirit . . . neither can He know them" (1 Corinthians 2:14). Discussing theology with someone who does not yet believe generally leads to fruitless arguments. The non-believing person will usually go to the mat to defend their position. There is an old saying, "A man convinced against his will, is of the same opinion still." As Paul emphasizes, "Faith comes by hearing and hearing by the Word of God" (Romans 10:17). Jesus is the Word of God, preach Him.

There is great value in the scriptural directive to demonstrate the love of God to all people, including one's enemies. Muting the Gospel because I feel it may make the other person uncomfortable honestly represents a failure on my part to love the other person. I've found that this is the thinking I have embraced at times, only to realize later that I was really more concerned about my discomfort in sharing the Gospel than I was in possibly offending the other person. In fact, not preaching the Gospel requires willful disobedience to the clear command of Jesus Himself. Matthew 28:19: "Go therefore and make disciples of all the nations, baptizing them in the name of the Father and of the Son and of the Holy Spirit."

It would be absurd to expect a person to become a disciple of Jesus and to be baptized without first hearing the Gospel. As Paul reasons, "How then shall they call on Him in whom they have not believed? And how shall they believe in Him of whom they have not heard? And how shall they hear without a preacher" (Romans 10:14).

Jesus continues:

"And this gospel of the kingdom will be preached in all the world as a witness to all the nations, and then the end will come" (Matthew 24:14). The fact that the preaching of the Gospel has been left up to us is obvious in that Jesus at the time of His death, burial, and resurrection had not gone into "all the world." He hands that assignment to us, His body on earth through the power of the Holy Spirit.

Paul writes in several places the necessity of preaching the Gospel, perhaps no more poignantly than in the following passage:

> But even if our gospel is veiled, it is veiled to those who are perishing, whose minds the god of this age has blinded, who do not believe, lest the light of the gospel of the glory of Christ, who is the image of God, should shine on them. For we do not preach ourselves, but Christ Jesus the Lord, and ourselves your bondservants for Jesus' sake. (2 Corinthians 4:3-5)

CHAPTER 2: "NEVER DISCUSS RELIGION OR POLITICS"

Notice Paul says, "For we do not preach ourselves, but Christ Jesus the Lord." We must preach the Gospel. Down through the centuries, the Gospel has been faithfully preached by believers like you and me. I know I'm generally "preaching to the choir" here, but I believe we need to once again be stirred up to share Christ with those we come in contact with casually or have a relationship with. I pray often for my family and friends, but find that I seldom speak of Jesus, and even less often do I purpose to share the Gospel with them. I make mention of the fact that I need boldness—just as we all do so that you reading this may know my heart on these issues. My purpose in writing this book is not to point the finger at others but to impart courage to all of us who purpose to be ambassadors for Christ. As ambassadors we are mandated to boldly preach the Gospel knowing that we will be rejected and scorned by some but will lead others to eternal life. I have led a few to salvation over the years, and I can tell you the joy that has come from those who came to salvation erases the memory of those who resisted the Good News. Our assignment is clear.

We must consciously resist being swayed by a culture that increasingly believes and spews out false narratives about our Lord and our faith, remembering that the truth will set the people free. The notion that justice can be achieved by more legislation and ideological training is both a false hope and a pipe dream. The scripture says in Jeremiah:

Thus says the Lord: "Cursed is the man who trusts in

AMERICA: LOST AND FOUND

man And makes flesh his strength, Whose heart departs from the Lord. Blessed is the man who trusts in the Lord, And whose hope is the Lord" (Jeremiah 17:5, 7).

The preaching of the Gospel is the only hope for mankind in a world that is spiraling into the chaos and a godless, hellish existence. But we have the true hope that every person needs. They, as we all once did, just don't know it yet.

Jesus gave us this promise, "He who believes in Me, as the Scripture has said, out of his heart will flow rivers of living water" (John 7:38). Let us determine to release the "living water" that is within all of us so that many will never thirst again and enter into the joy of the Lord.

OR POLITICS

There's no way around it. Politics, unless you're discussing it with those who agree with you, can be the catalyst for some pretty heated discourse. Here, I am referring to a political discussion between two people who ostensibly share a common belief system, as would be the case with two or more people who are of the Christian faith. In this case, you have common ground in your shared faith. But, as I've stated elsewhere, Christians can hold very different perspectives on how their faith should affect their sociological and political views. The goal, then, is to ensure, as much as it depends on you, that the outcome of the discussion makes clear what the Word of God says regarding the issue(s) and that all parties might agree with that conclusion.

CHAPTER 2: "NEVER DISCUSS RELIGION OR POLITICS"

GAME PLAN

If you find yourself in a situation where the conversation goes political, set your mind on being a good and sincerely interested listener. Giving the person whose political views are divergent from yours an honest hearing tells them that you respect them and their views, even if you vehemently disagree with them. This hopefully allows you to share your political views and opinions. What I always try to employ is speaking the truth in love. People on both sides of the aisle can be very strident in the presentation of their views. The last thing you want to engage in is a heated shouting match. Neither party will benefit from the outcome. If the person or persons you are engaged in discussion with begin to demonstrate high levels of emotion and passion about their positions, it can be very difficult not to respond in kind. But if you are convinced about what you believe, such as the truth contained in the Bible, you can draw from the peace you have that is not available to others. It is from this place that you tap into the ability to be respectful to the other person and share your beliefs and thoughts with passion and conviction, minus the angst. Always remember, "A soft answer turns away wrath" (Proverbs 15:1).

LOVE MEANS ACCEPTANCE AND APPROVAL, RIGHT?

If ever there was a topic in our current cultural environment that bridges not only "Religion" but "Politics" and has caused much-heated debate in the Body of Christ, the subject of "lifestyles" certainly tops the list. Love, according to 1 Corinthians 13:6-7, "does not rejoice in iniquity, but rejoices in the truth; bears all things, believes all things, hopes all things, endures all things."

Now does your acceptance of someone's opinions or behavior mean that you necessarily approve of them? Acceptance by def is the quality or state of being accepted or acceptable; the act of accepting something or someone: the fact of being accepted: APPROVAL (emphasis added).[1]

Accepting, or we could say, acknowledging the fact of another person's particular opinion or behaviors does not necessarily equate to approval of that opinion or those behaviors. Don't we all have loved ones who demonstrate behaviors, idiosyncrasies, and habits that we don't approve of or agree with, and yet our love and even devotion to them is unwavering? Newsflash: we all possess behaviors that others don't approve of. Even those acting out the worst behaviors one could ever imagine can be extended acceptance based on their intrinsic value of having been created in the image of God.

This, however, does not mean that a stamp of approval on abhorrent behavior is required to prove our acceptance of the value of each human life. That would require accepting and approving the acts of the Hitlers, Stalins, and Maos of the world. No, our acceptance of all persons is affirmed by the fact that they are created in God's likeness.

CHAPTER 2: "NEVER DISCUSS RELIGION OR POLITICS"

HOW WOKE ARE YOU?

Fast forward to our progressive "woke" culture and we find that mere acceptance of a person's chosen lifestyle is no longer adequate by current social mores. Forced approval and even programmed indoctrination are becoming more of a requirement, particularly as they relate to LGBTQ+ lifestyles. The pressure to endorse such lifestyles is so enormous that employers, public education, and even the military have made unlegislated additions of sexual preference and transgenderism to the "Title VII of the Civil Rights Act of 1964" anti-discrimination provisions, even though this is not required by the law itself.

But first what is it to be woke? The *Merriam-Webster Dictionary* defines *woke* as "aware of and actively attentive to important societal facts and issues (especially issues of racial and social justice)." But the reality is that woke is not a static but a fluid, subjective concept, depending on which side of the divide you stand. To leftists, including the mainstream media, it speaks of enlightenment and social justice. Conservatives, however, use it disparagingly, suggesting it to be another form of social conditioning. Critics have come to associate "wokeness" with political correctness, cancel culture, and left-leaning orientations.

Regardless of your stance, have you noticed how anyone, regardless of their societal stature or position who dares have an opposing view regarding the current paradigms of woke culture, is often labeled with a variety of subjective and often slanderous tags such as "homophobe," "transphobe," and the like?

A phobia is defined as "an intense, persistent, irrational fear of a specific object, activity, situation, or person that manifests in physical symptoms such as sweating, trembling, rapid heartbeat, or shortness of breath, and that motivates avoidance behavior."[2]

Now, disagreeing with a person's lifestyle choices does not equate to an "irrational fear." Usually, this has nothing to do with the motivation or belief system of the person being accused of such transgressions. The accusers, who are generally LGBTQ+ advocates, politicians, or the mainstream media, rarely have had any personal conversation with the accused to know their actual motivation and/or beliefs. For them, labels and accusations are a very convenient way to "nip in the bud" any opposing viewpoints regardless of how well-reasoned they may be. The goal of these advocates is not civilized discourse but rather a quelling and besmirching of those with opposing views.

Another tactic that has been commonly employed, particularly in social media platforms, is outright censorship through woke's cancel culture. Viewpoints that differ from the "accepted" or "approved" narrative are labeled "disinformation" and as listed above, tattooed with the usual labels by the usual suspects. We've all seen videos of question-and-answer sessions with brilliant speakers such as Jordan Peterson, Ben Shapiro, and Michael Knowles. Here, the interviewer poses the question, or rather a statement of position, and is given a well-reasoned, logical,

CHAPTER 2: "NEVER DISCUSS RELIGION OR POLITICS"

and sensible answer by the interviewee, only to receive an emotional outburst and, again, a plethora of labeling.

To their credit, I have never heard any of the above-mentioned speakers respond in kind, even to the most vitriolic of detractors. However, the proponents of the various strains of "wokeism" view any disagreement with their views as some form of phobic response that couldn't possibly be rational and, therefore, must be the result of racism, transphobia, or homophobia. In other words, if you disagree with them, your only possible motivation must be hate. The possibility that those who disagree with them could still respect them as fellow human beings by the belief that we have all been created in God's own image seems to be outside their paradigm.

For instance, those pursuing a homosexual lifestyle who are confronted with biblical passages that condemn the practice sometimes attempt to use scripture itself to answer the charge. "But didn't Jesus Himself say to the woman caught in adultery that He didn't condemn her?" Yes, He did say that, but the rest of the verse, whether in ignorance or on purpose, is routinely overlooked, which is "go and sin no more." Did Jesus accept the woman based on her repentant posture? Absolutely. Was He approving of her behavior? Absolutely not, as the whole verse makes plain. This reminds me of someone else, revealed in the Bible, who often attempted to misuse scripture!

There are, sadly, those even in pastoral positions who wish to justify homosexual practice, saying that Jesus Himself never explicitly condemned the behavior. But you must understand that as the second Person of the Godhead and the "Word of God" incarnate, He was as much a revelator of the passages that condemn homosexuality as the Father and the Holy Spirit. He was also a present participant in the destruction of Sodom and Gomorrah. Jesus did not have to expound on every form of sin to prove that He did not agree with it.

Since my goal is to encourage and, to some degree, provide education for people of faith to stand unwaveringly in their belief in and practice of the Word of God, it is crucial that as many of us as possible be in agreement. We should not allow fear to mute us when we know what the Word says concerning any given issue. We just must remain committed to speaking the truth in love.

CHAPTER 3
"MOMMY, DID I REALLY COME FROM A MONKEY?"

Now that we've exposed our current culture of compromise on God's truths, let's move into some assessments of where we are as a nation. What beliefs are the predominant markers of American thought and values? My view is that if the enemy has succeeded at anything, it is in the realm of controlling the narrative in several major spheres of our culture. Education, government, and the media certainly play a dominant role in what is and isn't morally acceptable. Did I miss something? How about church?

DECEPTIVE CATCHWORDS

The enemy has also made great strides in convincing many church leaders to bow at the altar of humanism and secularism in an attempt to appear "relevant." If you have any doubt about that, just count how churches display "pride" flags and espouse woke slogans like "Love is Love," "Black

Lives Matter," and "Science is Real." All these statements appeal to a sense of solidarity and acceptance. But they are in fact thinly veiled, ungodly deceptions that those who do not hold to "sound doctrine" readily embrace. They believe that in being inclusive, they are taking the moral high ground. Just because someone or something is loved by someone else does not validate it as being a true expression of love. In the extreme, Adolph Hitler loved exterminating Jews, homosexuals, and anyone he considered inferior to the Arian Race. Can you see the rabbit hole that claiming "Love is Love" can be—i.e., justifying anyone's behavior if it is done in the name of love? This phrase is primarily used in the context of people with same-sex attraction. But then, where do you draw the line? The Bible draws the line!

Of course, Black Lives Matter. According to the Bible, all lives matter and are of equal value because all of mankind has been created by God. "So, God created man in His own image; in the image of God, He created him; male and female He created them" (Genesis 1:27).

The inference is that our nation, as a whole, does not place the same value on the lives of Americans of African descent as it does on those of Caucasian descent. This is a gross presumption that is often ascribed to the entire non-black population in America.

Are there people in our country who believe that people of color are of less value than themselves? Of course, there are. By the way, the inverse is true as well, but that hardly qualifies it as an overarching characteristic of the

CHAPTER 3: "MOMMY, DID I REALLY COME FROM A MONKEY?"

American people, white or black. No one I know holds this view of their fellow human beings. In fact, I have never heard anyone in my academic, workplace, or social spheres espouse such a belief. Yet to listen to much of the rhetoric presented as news, you can't help but believe that "systemic racism" is the norm here.

THE FRUIT OF EVOLUTIONARY THINKING

So what is the real fuel for this kind of ideological fire? The fire that has been kindled, I believe, is perhaps due to the most influential belief system responsible for opening the Pandora's Box of people embracing the idea that they can be a law unto themselves without eternal consequence. That belief system is called "Evolution."

Because of my sensitivity to the subject, I often notice that the term "evolved" is commonly used in the everyday vernacular to describe the increased complexity of everything from cars to computers. Think about that for a moment. Would you ever consider buying a car that the salesman described as being the result of random chance and natural processes over and against a car that was the result of ingenious design, sophisticated engineering, and high-tech manufacturing processes? Yet this term is so ingrained in the vocabulary of our culture that we hardly notice it. Would we ever believe that a massively complex machine, such as an automobile, just arrived, as a result of its own making, having a multitude of specific and integrated functions for specific and integrated purposes without having a highly intelligent and intentional designer?

Consider the human species. Let's park here for a moment. Jumping past the marvel that is the human body, the fact that we are not mere physical machines but living beings that can see, perceive, think about what we see and perceive and interact with the world we live in adds exponential complexity to our existence. We are human *beings*, not just human bodies. Now the human body, by itself, is virtually incomprehensible in its complexity. An amalgamation of organs, each with a specific function and purpose, which must then interact in concert with the numerous other systems of the body, each with their specific function and purpose, resulting in an integrated living body. I believe that the sheer intellect required to grasp this complexity is rare among us and is one of the explanations for why so many ostensibly "brilliant" scientists and academics hold to such an untenable and scientifically improvable explanation of origins as evolution. Like so many of us, they simply can't grasp the miracle of human life. So we and they tend to reach for the low-hanging fruit of what seems to be a plausible explanation.

The quest for a sense of purpose, meaning, and value is a strong mental and emotional drive within all human beings. I remember a song named "Is That All There Is?" by Peggy Lee in 1969 which lamented the fact that all the pleasures, accomplishments, relationships, and wealth one accumulates in life, in the end, still leave you empty and bereft of meaning. Occasionally I come up with what I feel

CHAPTER 3: "MOMMY, DID I REALLY COME FROM A MONKEY?"

are great ideas for bumper stickers. Remember the bumper sticker that goes "He who dies with the most toys wins?" I would have changed it to "He who dies with the most toys is still dead." Okay, maybe not.

Belief in evolution to the exclusion of a Creator leaves us in a hopeless state of meaningless existence only to one day have our life and very being extinguished with the death of the body. In contrast, knowing that you were created with design and purpose and that you are not just the result of random natural processes renders the mere pursuit of worldly goods and temporal pleasures as ends unto themselves far less attractive and meaningful. Does not possessing the knowledge that you were designed and created for an eternal purpose by a benevolent Creator elevate all that you do? Doesn't it give your life exponentially greater meaning and eternal value? The subject of origins is an area that the enemy has successfully used to confuse and bring into question who we are intrinsically and where we came from.

In 1925 the infamous Scopes trial took place in Dayton, TN. The State of Tennessee vs. John Thomas Scopes pitted two high-profile attorneys, William Jennings Bryant and Clarence Darrow, against each other. Bryant represented the State of Tennessee for the prosecution, and Darrow represented Scopes for the defense. The following excerpt describes the premise of the trial:

AMERICA: LOST AND FOUND

THE SCOPES TRIAL: A BATTLE BETWEEN CREATIONISM AND EVOLUTION IN PUBLIC SCHOOLS

The Scopes "Monkey" Trial (the official name is State of Tennessee v John Thomas Scopes) began on July 10, 1925, in Dayton, Tennessee. On trial was science teacher John T. Scopes, charged with violating the Butler Act, which prohibited the teaching of evolution in Tennessee public schools.

Known in its day as "the trial of the century," the Scopes Trial pitted two famous lawyers against one another: Beloved orator and three-time presidential candidate William Jennings Bryan for the prosecution and renowned trial attorney Clarence Darrow for the defense.

On July 21, Scopes was found guilty and fined $100, but the fine was revoked a year later during the appeal to the Tennessee Supreme Court. As the first trial was broadcast live on radio in the United States, the Scopes trial brought widespread attention to the controversy over creationism versus evolution.[1]

A year later, the decision was appealed to the Tennessee Supreme Court, and the lower court's ruling was upheld. The law stayed in effect until it was ruled unconstitutional by the United States Supreme Court in 1968.

Since the Scopes trial, and the subsequent US Supreme Court ruling, a slow and steady shift has occurred in American culture. As evolution gained traction as the "scientific" explanation of origins, we have gradually seen

CHAPTER 3: "MOMMY, DID I REALLY COME FROM A MONKEY?"

ourselves more as a product of evolutionary processes known as "natural selection," rather than the result of a Creator designing and forming us after His own image and likeness. This has given rise to all kinds of questionable notions as to our nature, value, and responsibility, or lack thereof, as human beings.

The idea that we are the result of nothing more than an infinite number of chemical reactions and the resulting natural processes with no expectation of having to answer to an eternal Judge has given rise to numerous godless ideologies, which have been responsible for the death of hundreds of millions of people in the last two centuries. Marxism, which led to socialism and communism, was the prevailing political philosophy behind the creation of the gulags and great slaughters in the Soviet Union, as well as the Cultural Revolution in Mao's China. It is estimated that in these two regimes alone upwards of 120 million people perished. Both regimes proudly claimed there is no God. They did, however, believe in the Soviet Union, and still hold the belief, in the case of China and other totalitarian countries, that "the end justifies the means." In their thinking, the fact that they were "successful" in removing all who were resistant to their authority and power justifies the genocide and atrocities committed to achieve those ends. Stalin and Mao must have been more than a little undone as they stood before their Creator for judgment.

This is the fruit of rejecting the truth that we are created beings answerable to a just Creator and believing the lie that we are only the product of evolutionary processes.

The theory of evolution has long enjoyed preeminence as *the* "scientific model" for explaining origins. This is quite interesting, since the scientific method requires observation and repeatability over time to establish something as a fact of nature. Evolution cannot fulfill either of these conditions of the scientific method to establish it as factual. And yet it has been and still is ostensibly presented as fact from elementary school through university as the unquestionable explanation of why and how everything exists. Isn't it telling that Evolution, which is almost universally accepted as the force in nature to explain all that exists, is still called a theory? Doesn't it seem a lot to ask that we trust the cause and outcome of our existence to an idea that can never be scientifically proven?

But then the evolutionist will counter by saying that you can't prove that God exists either. To believe this statement, one must engage in willful ignorance. If we objectively examine various aspects of the physical universe we should, and do, arrive at the conclusion that the physical cosmos and life itself display a dizzying level of design complexity. This complexity must and does work together to make life even possible. Without the physical laws by which the universe operates, we would have nothing but massive random chaos. Celestial bodies would move aimlessly out of control, often colliding with catastrophic results. Not exactly the environment needed to foster the development of organized life, is it! And remember we still haven't explained where the cosmos and life came from. Notice that evolution always starts

CHAPTER 3: "MOMMY, DID I REALLY COME FROM A MONKEY?"

with existing material but is incapable of explaining where it came from.

I remember reading a humorous scenario where a group of scientists proudly approached God saying that He was no longer needed as they had figured out how to create life. God replied, "Really, show Me how you do it?"

One of the scientists confidently replied, "Well, first we take some dirt and . . ."

At this point, God interrupts and says, "Wait a minute, make your own dirt."

IS IT REALLY SCIENCE?

Although you rarely hear it admitted in most "scientific journals," there are a substantial number of credible and respected scientists who have come to question the tenets of evolution and its plausibility to explain the origin of life.

Excerpts from the following article "Over 1,000 Scientists Openly Dissent from Evolution Theory" comes from *New American* magazine online, March 19, 2019:

> Over 1,000 doctoral scientists from around the world have signed a "Dissent" statement expressing skepticism about Darwin's evolution theory, sparking fresh controversy over an idea that is at the core of many people's worldview. The significant announcement, made last month, has been all but ignored by the establishment media. But it is making waves nevertheless.

AMERICA: LOST AND FOUND

The dissenting scientists all united around one simple statement. "We are skeptical of claims for the ability of random mutation and natural selection to account for the complexity of life," the Ph.D.s said. "Careful examination of the evidence for Darwinian theory should be encouraged. There is scientific dissent from Darwinism. It deserves to be heard."

And many of the scientists speaking out about this are prominent and highly respected. More than a dozen of the signatories, for instance, are members of various national academies of science, including those in the United States, Russia, Hungary, the Czech Republic, and other nations, as well as the Royal Society.

More than a few come from America's most prestigious universities such as Harvard, MIT, Princeton, and Yale. Others come from prestigious foreign universities and research institutions such as the University of Cambridge, London's Natural History Museum, Moscow State University, Hong Kong University, University of Stellenbosch in South Africa, Institut de Paléontologie Humaine in France, Ben-Gurion University in Israel, and more.

The experts speaking out also represent a broad array of scientific disciplines and fields. These include molecular biology, biochemistry, biology, entomology, computational quantum chemistry, microbiology, psychiatry, behavioral sciences, astrophysics, marine biology, cellular biology, physics, astronomy, math, geology, anthropology, and many more. Many medical doctors are raising questions, too.

CHAPTER 3: "MOMMY, DID I REALLY COME FROM A MONKEY?"

Beyond the scientific aspects, there are also profound implications of the theory. One reason religious humanists such as public-education Founding Father John Dewey latched on to it so fervently is because it allowed them to exclude the existence of a Creator. America's Founding Fathers held as a "self-evident" "truth" that man was created, and endowed by that Creator with certain rights. Humanists such as Dewey and his cohorts, who designed the modern public-school system, rejected that—along with the concept of unalienable, God-given rights that governments exist to protect.

Regardless of what one thinks about the evolution theory, it is still a theory. To force Americans who disagree with this controversial theory to fund its propagation in taxpayer-funded government schools—especially when no alternative is even allowed to be mentioned, and when the implications are so huge—is immoral and wrong. Parents and taxpayers should take a lesson from these courageous scientists and speak out.[2]

It is also interesting to find out that there is extreme peer pressure and even "persecution" against any scientist who dares to buck the "evolutionary" party line. Wouldn't you think that after centuries of pet scientific beliefs going by the wayside, such as "the earth is flat" and "air has no substance," that the scientific community would be more inclined to recognize that new discoveries are an ongoing occurrence and should be expected? Sadly, many beliefs are held onto with near-religious fervor and are not easily relinquished to the point of absurdity. Such is the case with the theory of evolution.

And why is evolution so vehemently held onto and still propagated? I'm sure there are many arguments as to why this is, but my own "theory" is the very reason why, before becoming a Christian, I believed in evolution. If I evolved, then I wouldn't need to believe in a God that I might be accountable to. The scripture doesn't say without good cause that "The heart of man is deceitful above all things and desperately wicked; who can know it" (Jeremiah 17:9).

The last paragraph of the article just quoted reveals the underlying intent and the ideology of those who tenaciously hold onto the belief that evolution is still the universal process at work and that it is still the most scientific explanation for life on earth. One phrase here "to exclude the existence of a Creator" reveals its intent is to remove any vestige of the belief in an intelligent Creator and to replace it with the ideology that we are merely products of natural processes with no unalienable rights. Can you imagine the horrors such a philosophy of existence precipitates? As previously mentioned, nations that have adopted this type of godless ideology in the last 120 or so years have accounted for tens of millions of deaths through wars, purges, and ethnic cleansing.

The conflicting belief systems at work in the world today, and throughout history, are between those who believe mankind has a Creator who has endowed us with unalienable rights and to whom we are accountable and those who do not. Those who do not believe in a Creator, whether knowingly or not, cede their inalienable rights to secular human governments whose motivations are rarely altruistic and are seldom designed to benefit the citizen. In the most basic terms, they are the belief systems of the godly vs. the ungodly.

CRIME

There is also, I believe, a direct correlation between the increased secularist worldview and the continuing occurrence of violent crime in America. In all categories of lawlessness, from relatively minor offenses to the most horrific and evil crimes, the total number of crimes committed per total population does not diminish over time as would be expected if we are truly evolving and getting better.

The Bible has the answer to this: "Where there is no revelation, the people cast off restraint; but happy is he who keeps the law" (Proverbs 29:18).

It is clear that the most glaring blind spot in secularist and humanist ideologies is the failure, and even refusal, to recognize the fallen nature of mankind. They view humankind, as they view the rest of nature, as being in the process of continual evolution. That means we are all getting better as we evolve to a higher state of being. But when you consider a subject such as lawlessness, the evidence is clear. We, as a society, are not getting better. We are degenerating into a far more lawless, increasingly violent, and anarchical people.

AMERICA: LOST AND FOUND

Secular psychology claims that we are just a product of our environment and that our circumstances of birth and the societal strata of our upbringing are the major determinants of the kind of people we will become. This overrides the view of intentional choices made by thinking human beings. See the article cited below for more information.[3] Lawyers use this type of ideology to argue for reduced sentences and even acquittals for their clients. The child's famous excuse "The devil made me do it!" has been replaced with an equally fallacious excuse "The family, neighborhood, or school I went to, etc. . . . made me do it."

As a result, the attempted removal of personal responsibility and accountability has risen to the level of a societal disease which only serves to embolden the individual to engage in antisocial behavior without conscience, regret, or even remorse.

This kind of paradigm is far removed from the worldview our nation held for much of its existence based on the paradigm: "What a man sows, that shall he reap." The word of God makes it clear that the seeds a person chooses to sow will produce a like harvest, be it good or evil.

The social scientist could very well postulate that perhaps people could be at different stages of the evolutionary process and that this would account for the vastly different value systems that people operate in. This, of course, would present major problems affecting the whole theory of evolution. How would you explain contemporaries of the human species operating at seemingly varying stages of development? I would argue that you can't because

CHAPTER 3: "MOMMY, DID I REALLY COME FROM A MONKEY?"

the whole premise of the theory of evolution is untenable in the first place. The issues that arise from embracing evolution are numerous, and you only have ten fingers to plug up the ever-increasing number of holes in the dike. An archaeologist and former atheist once said, "Evolution doesn't just have a missing link that we need to find, we're missing the chain, sprocket, and the entire bicycle."

No, evolution isn't science, and you didn't come from a monkey. To believe that life was spontaneously generated due to random chance, electrochemical reactions, and complex development via genetic mutations (the vast majority of which are lethal to any living organism and are not repeatable) and then organized itself into levels of complexity that would take a computer to calculate requires incredible faith. The factual and observable evidence for this kind of thinking simply does not exist. It's quite telling that the evolutionist considers those who believe in Jesus Christ to be the ones following improvable myths when it is the Christian faith that is built, far and away, upon the most substantial eyewitness and historical evidence of any major event in ancient history. If the theory of evolution had anything approaching that kind of evidence, then maybe we would have something reasonable to talk about.

> Some things are believed because they are demonstrably true, but many other things are believed simply because they have been asserted repeatedly and repetition has been accepted as a substitute for evidence. (Thomas Sowell)[4]

CHAPTER 4
WHOSE BODY IS IT?

Certainly, the greatest national disgrace and outright sin that has ever occurred in America is the abortion of over 60 million preborn human beings. With the 1973 Supreme Court decision of Roe vs. Wade, abortion was codified to become a legal practice in the United States. Even with this decision, the language was ambiguous as to when life actually begins. Justice Blackman, who wrote the Opinion of the Court, says this, "We need not resolve the difficult question of when life begins. When those trained in the respective disciplines of medicine, philosophy, and theology are unable to arrive at any consensus, the judiciary, at this point in the development of man's knowledge, is not in a position to speculate as to the answer" (p160).[1]

This statement is little more than an appeal to ignorance as to whether or not abortion is in fact the taking of a human life. Ruling in favor of legalizing it, over and against exercising discretion to protect that life until the question of when life begins could be scientifically resolved, reveals the ideological bias that drove the decision.

CHAPTER 4: WHOSE BODY IS IT?

And what have been the results?

1. African American and Hispanic women account for 55.4% of abortions.
2. 58% of women are ages 20-28.
3. 85% of women obtaining an abortion are unmarried.
4. 60% have already given birth to one or more children.
5. 37% identify themselves as evangelical or Catholic.
6. 75% of women are low-income and are near or below the poverty line.[2]

Several things are disturbing about these statistics:

1. Over half of the abortions obtained yearly are among African American and Hispanic women. Considering these groups represent approximately 30% of the women in America, this percentage is highly disproportionate to the total female population.
2. Seventy-five percent of women are among the poorest sectors of the American population. Margaret Sanger, founder of Planned Parenthood, has a notorious history of allegedly placing birth control facilities in poor and minority neighborhoods. She drew much attention to herself due to advocating for eugenics, "the practice or advocacy of controlled selective breeding of human populations (as by sterilization) to improve the population's genetic composition."[3]

The following statement reveals her belief in the inferiority of African Americans. "She believed that only the 'fit' should be breeding and that family size should be limited. Sanger particularly targeted the black population through her 'Negro Project,' calling African Americans 'reckless breeders' and 'human weeds.'"[4]

Of late, Planned Parenthood has attempted to distance itself from its founder's racist reproductive philosophies, which until now have been allowed to stand and even embraced. There are numerous organizations, public and private, that exist to help alleviate the poor from their state by providing higher education, trade schools, and financial assistance. It seems radical indeed to engage in practices whose solution to eradicating poverty is to abort the next generation of "poor Americans."

The entire argument for abortion being an acceptable and legal form of birth control hinges on the false assumption that life does not begin at conception but at various other stages of development.

However, according to the American College of Pediatricians:

The predominance of human biological research confirms that human life begins at conception—fertilization. At fertilization, the human being emerges as a whole, genetically distinct, individuated zygotic living human organism, a member of the species *Homo sapiens*, needing only the proper environment in order to grow and develop. The difference between the individual in its adult

CHAPTER 4: WHOSE BODY IS IT?

stage and in its zygotic stage is one of form, not nature. This statement focuses on the scientific evidence of when an individual human life begins.[5]

Consider the following argument appealing to the science of reproduction,

Tara Sander Lee, Senior Fellow and Director of Life Sciences at the Charlotte Lozier Institute, stated, "Life begins from the moment of conception when the sperm fertilizes the egg, because there is the creation of a new, totally distinct, integrated organism or a human being, which is going to be biologically distinct from all other life forms on this planet." The first cell is biologically distinct because it has its own DNA that is different from either biological parent and all other humans.[6]

Numerous scientific resources confirm this conclusion. A quick search as to "when life begins" will reveal overwhelming scientific consensus that life begins at conception.[7]

Justice Blackman may not have known when life begins, but those to whom he appeals to resolve the question have emphatically clarified the answer to this question. *Life begins at conception!*

On the other hand, the shrieking cry of those in the streets and of those on the radical left was, at that time, and can still be heard today, is, "It's my body. I have the right to do with it whatever I want." Well, as it turns out,

43

the person in your womb is a separate and distinct member of the *Homo sapiens* species. You therefore do not have the "right" to destroy someone else's body.

However, you do have the right to take the necessary precautions to prevent becoming pregnant. If you choose not to avail yourself of such precautions, the only right you then have is to accept responsibility for your actions and deliver the child within you. You then have the right to raise your child or give it up for adoption to a family that appreciates the value of the child and will raise it lovingly and responsibly.

The Bible, as well as science, makes it perfectly clear whose body is whose:

> The Lord has called Me from the womb; from the matrix of My mother He has made mention of My name (Isaiah 49:1). Before I formed you in the womb I knew you. Before you were born I sanctified you; I ordained you a prophet to the nations (Jeremiah 1:5).

Another attempt to justify abortion at various stages of the pregnancy is the concept of viability. Does the developing child have the ability to survive outside the mother's womb? Different demarcations have been put forth to determine viability, such as physical movements, hand grasping, the first detection of a heartbeat, and so on. Of course, the proponents of abortion can't come to a consensus as to which "marker" should be the determining factor to establish viability. In other words, trying to

CHAPTER 4: WHOSE BODY IS IT?

determine viability is completely arbitrary. These "markers of viability" assume the absence of personhood until some predetermined event during pregnancy, thus ignoring the accepted scientific fact that life begins at conception. How "viable" is a one- or two-year-old outside the mother's womb without the necessary nurture and care needed to survive?

These ideas expose a disposition toward expediency rather than moral principles. They attempt to alleviate personal responsibility for engaging in sexual intercourse merely for pleasure's sake, willfully ignoring the possible and natural outcome, which is reproduction. How irresponsible and cold-hearted it is to be sexually active and flaunt the idea that "if I get pregnant, I can just kill the result by having an abortion!" This criminally lazy thought process is even more repugnant considering the plethora of birth control options that are available to avoid the question of having an abortion in the first place.

Consider the following excerpt from the article "Should Abortion Be Legal?"

> Upon fertilization, a human individual is created with a unique genetic identity that remains unchanged throughout his or her life. This individual has a fundamental right to life, which must be protected. Jerome Lejeune, the French geneticist who discovered the chromosome abnormality that causes Down syndrome, stated: "To accept the fact that after fertilization has taken place a new human has come into being is no longer a matter

of taste or opinion. . . . The human nature of the human being from conception to old age is not a metaphysical contention, it is plain experimental evidence.[8]

It is now even being asserted that a child can be legally terminated after birth under "certain circumstances." The proper term for this is *infanticide*. It is also known as the *barbaric* embodiment of evil.

Another argument regularly put forth to justify having an abortion is in the cases of rape and incest.

I emphatically agree that these are heinous crimes and are horrible violations for any woman to suffer. The perpetrators of such crimes should be subject to very severe sentencing requirements. I confess that in the past I passively considered abortion to be justified in such instances, sympathizing with the women who had been so victimized. But the innocent must not be the ones—in this case, the preborn child—to incur the punishment in place of the guilty by having their life taken from them. I also believe that a just society will provide for the financial, medical, emotional, and spiritual needs of the women we are asking to carry their child to delivery. Should a woman not wish to raise her child, there are always numerous couples who want very badly to adopt a child as their own. For me as a Christian, the most troubling statistic is that 37% of the women having abortions claim to be evangelical or Catholic. If we do not live out what we say we believe, what does that make us?

Before engaging in sexual intercourse, the man and the woman should appreciate the fact that the natural and

CHAPTER 4: WHOSE BODY IS IT?

obvious outcome of their actions may very well be pregnancy. If this is not their desired outcome, then responsible means to prevent pregnancy must be utilized. Abortion, as a "safety net" to abrogate this responsibility, should not even be a consideration.

Adoption, not abortion, is the just solution. The result of abortion, aside from taking a life, is not just the alleviation of an "inconvenient situation," it is often the beginning of a terrible sense of guilt and regret for many women. Only those with a dark and hardened heart will feel no remorse for what they have done. For the Christian or any moral person for that matter, it must be clearly understood that abortion is not a choice, it is premeditated murder! The contention that a woman has the right to determine what she does with her body, including aborting her child, is neither moral from a scriptural view nor scientific. It is not her body that suffers the abortion! The child in the womb is not just another appendage of the mother's body. It is a completely separate individual whose life must be protected in the process of its development. That process can continue from conception to a person's early twenties to reach full development. Consider this question; which day of your physical life, from conception until now, is any less necessary to the continuity of your existence than any other?

Volumes of legislation have been put forth to either prevent or protect abortion. Those on the far left will tirelessly fight to keep abortion available to any woman who wants it. In the past, bills have been written requiring women to have an ultrasound and view the growing child in their wombs. When the procedure has been applied, a high percentage of the women, upon seeing and recognizing that they are looking at their baby and not just a "blob" of cellular tissue, choose not to go through with the abortion. I have long held that one of the main reasons why so many women and their partners were willing to go through with having an abortion was due to little more than the adage—"Out of sight, out of mind." The results of the ultrasound procedure certainly lend credence to this idea. And oh, did the abortion lobby throw a hissy fit over such a "violation" of the woman's right to choose. It appears that those who were pro-abortion recognized the powerful effect the image of a living, growing, and recognizable baby had on women, and they did everything they could to keep it "out of sight and out of mind."

As previously stated, this is a horrific and disgraceful blot in the history of our country. Others may feel that slavery, racial injustice, the treatment of Native Americans, and even the use of the atomic bomb against the Japanese are the worst stains in our history. I agree that these represent the dark side of America's past and should never be forgotten or minimized. But, as a matter of sheer scale, nothing in our history remotely compares with the legalized infanticide called abortion, which has caused the death of over 60 million preborn human beings. This is virtually the same number of deaths that Adolph Hitler and the Axis powers have been attributed responsibility for in the entirety of World War II!

CHAPTER 5
OF THE CHILDREN

Train up a child in the way he should go, and when he is old he will not depart from it (Proverbs 22:6).

On the parenting front, society in general and the "educational system" in particular, have embraced what was termed in the 1960s as permissive parenting. This was to a large extent influenced by Dr. Benjamin Spock.[1] The idea is that we don't want to suppress little Johnny or Janie's creativity and inquisitiveness by inflicting oppressive rules and regulations upon them that restrict their behavior. The resultant decades of the endless increase in all sorts of crime, divorce, sexually transmitted diseases, and of late the propagation of transgenderism is a testament to our refusal as a society to train our children in the way they should go. It's our failure to teach them that they are personally responsible before God and society for their actions and that they will suffer life-diminishing consequences for those actions.

Observing the actions of many who have been raised within this "permissive paradigm," we are led to wonder if these folks ever heard the word *NO* in their upbringing.

If you have ever been to a park or any other public area where children are present, you have probably observed parents who have absolutely no control over their children's behavior.

If you are a good and responsible parent, you do not pat little Johnny or Janie on the head when they behave badly and just chalk it up to, "Well that's just what kids do" and "I certainly don't want to suppress their self-expression." Instead, lovingly correct the behavior, explaining to the child why the behavior was wrong and making it clear that there will be consequences if the behavior happens again. This is the behavioral discipline that will be required for any measure of the child's achievement and success in life. Also, you must then be willing to make good on your promise of consequences, or the child will quickly realize that you do not mean what you say and will continue repeating the undesired behavior.

Consider again what the Bible tells us about childhood training:

> Train up a child in the way he should go, and when he old he will not depart from it (Proverbs 22:6).
> The rod and rebuke give wisdom, but a child left to himself brings shame to his mother.... Correct your son, and he will give you rest; yes, he will give delight to your soul (Proverbs 29:15, 17).

A lot more could be said on this topic, and there are many excellent books on parenting that are available,

CHAPTER 5: OF THE CHILDREN

but we must be moving on to other pressing topics at this point.

"GOD'S CHILDREN ARE NOT FOR SALE"

Sadly, throughout history, there is nothing new about children being used as a commodity and enslaved. At best, they're used as forced labor, serving those greedy for riches by any means available, and at the absolute worst, they're used as sex slaves, forced to suffer the despicable and deviant lusts of primarily adult men. Jesus issues one of His sternest warnings regarding the treatment of children:

> But whoever causes one of these little ones who believe in Me to stumble, it would be better for him if a millstone were hung around his neck, and he were thrown into the sea. (Mark 9:42)

On July 4, 2023, the movie *The Sound of Freedom* was released. The salient slogan "God's children are not for sale" was coined by the movie's main character, Tim Ballard, played by Jim Caviezel. The entire film and media industries were shocked at the immediate box-office success of the film, outperforming all of Hollywood's concurrent "blockbuster" releases, and this, despite not having spent millions on prerelease promotion. In fact, the film had a relatively modest advertising budget, and the main means of promotion were via social media and word of mouth. I certainly told many people that this film was a must-see.

The upshot of this revealed that there is a substantial percentage of the population, not only in America but in many other countries as well, that have great concern regarding the extent of this evil in our midst. Thousands, including myself, have been motivated to take action by supporting organizations that physically and/or legislatively are fighting to expose and eradicate this despicable industry. Many others have decided to get directly involved in the fight. Of course, the foundation of the fight has been and continues to be in intercessory prayer, using the authority given to us by Jesus:

> And I will give you the keys of the kingdom of heaven, and whatever you bind on earth will be bound in heaven, and whatever you loose on earth will be loosed in heaven (Matthew 16:19).
>
> Behold, I give you the authority to trample on serpents and scorpions, and over all the power of the enemy, and nothing shall by any means hurt you (Luke 10:19).

The sex trafficking of children is but one of many tragic results of the United States Government refusing to secure our southern border. That "America the Beautiful" has become the worldwide hub for sex trafficking breaks my heart. For decades now, our country has been endlessly hailed as representing a progressive society by the "elite" in academia, politics, and media. In the stampede to remove

CHAPTER 5: OF THE CHILDREN

God from every public expression, including removing Him from our collective conscience, the current state of our society would be more accurately termed "regressive," as it descends into a never-ending abyss of human degradation. This is the absolute antithesis of the Founding Fathers' vision of "life, liberty, and the pursuit of happiness."

Here are a few of the facts surrounding the practice of sex trafficking as reported by the humanitarian organization "Save the Children":

> FACT: Trafficking can involve force, but people can also be trafficked through threats, coercion, or deception. People in trafficking situations can be controlled through drug addiction, violent relationships, manipulation, lack of financial independence, or isolation from family or friends, in addition to physical restraint or harm.
>
> FACT: Human trafficking can include forced labor, domestic servitude, organ trafficking, debt bondage, recruitment of children of child soldiers, and/or sex trafficking and forced prostitution.
>
> FACT: Trafficking occurs all over the world, though the most common forms of trafficking can differ by country. The United States is one of the most active sex trafficking countries in the world, where exploitation of trafficking victims occurs in cities, suburban and rural areas. (emphasis added)[2]

It is instructive to see the media's overall treatment of the *Sound of Freedom*. The usual suspects in the "mainstream media" responded not with empathy and outrage over the exposure of a horrendous evil but with a measure of skepticism, even attempting to denigrate the veracity of the film—which, by the way, was an accurate and factual docudrama about what actually happened.

There has been much outcry in the last several years about this type of documentary being little more than the propagation of conspiracy theories. The irony is that this tack of negative labeling now seems more applicable to those using it than to those to whom they attempt to apply it.

Let's continue to pray and declare that "God's Children Are Not for Sale."

LET'S GET EDUCATED

The situation in the public school system has become desperate. For decades, teachers and administrators have been hamstrung from disciplining students for bad behavior, which creates an unruly environment, hindering the quality and quantity of meaningful education. Schools have become places where truly "the inmates are running the asylum."

In the 1950s, the most serious disciplinary offenses in public schools involved talking in class and chewing gum. Now teachers are dealing with drugs, weapons being brought into class, and having profanities yelled at them by students who have never been required to show respect to their parents, teachers, or classmates. Scores

CHAPTER 5: OF THE CHILDREN

of responsible, dedicated, and quality teachers have been driven to either accept less pay, in some instances, at private schools, or leave the profession altogether rather than live with the dysfunctionality resident within public education.

The following article relates the reasons why and the sentiments of an ever-increasing number of educators who have left the field in recent years:

"THE NEW NORM IN K-12 PUBLIC SCHOOLS"

There was endless talk among educators nationwide during the early months of the pandemic in the Spring of 2020—Things couldn't and wouldn't go back to how it was before. The outdated and ineffective K-12 education system was exposed with increased clarity, and even educators realized it wasn't working as intended. Too many kids were falling through the cracks of the one-size-fits-all factory model system.

These noble conversations centered on the use of technology to enhance student learning, providing more personalized instruction, varying assessments, and so on. However, as we near the two-year mark since COVID's debut, K-12 public schools nationwide find that the approach to learning has not changed much despite the grand talk.

But while the ineffective learning practices have remained constant, much has, in fact, changed in K-12 public school environments. Unfortunately, these changes were not all for the best. Instead of improving academics, woke political priorities took center stage. In place of essential teacher training and professional development centered on the goal of enhancing student learning, teachers and staff were "trained" in Critical Race Theory, social-emotional learning, and the redefinition of gender, history, and core academic truths (even basic mathematical truths such as 2+2=4).

It's no wonder school administrators, teachers, and staff are fleeing and retiring early at record rates. Educators entered the profession to make a positive impact on the lives of students. When kids don't show up, or come to school full of anger, depression, or anxiety, a teacher's ability to engage students in learning is exponentially more challenging. Managing the emotions and harsh realities of their students' home lives fits the job description of a social worker, one for which teachers are neither prepared nor qualified to fulfill."[3]

Over the last several decades, the ungodly secularization of public education has been a growing cause of concern. The advent of the COVID-19 crisis, however, caused parents to become frighteningly aware, via the internet classroom, as to the extent of how ungodly, un-American, and outright immoral the curriculum being foisted upon our youth has become. Inappropriate sexual material for children beginning in kindergarten has been revealed! Much of this material, in the form of books and videos, is outright pornography. Seventy-five years ago,

CHAPTER 5: OF THE CHILDREN

few in America would have believed that such depravity in our public educational system could ever be allowed. Yet this is the reality in numerous school districts across the country, and we have not even mentioned the depths to which a majority of our universities have sunk in regards to rejecting biblical and traditional values. The negative influence of our educational system, particularly at the college level, is alarming. Consider the following statistics from Barna Research:

"WILL YOU KEEP YOUR FAITH IN COLLEGE?"

Odds are you won't, at least according to Barna Research. Barna estimates that roughly 70% of high school students who enter college as professing Christians will leave with little to no faith. These students usually don't return to their faith even after graduation, as Barna projects that

80% of those reared in the church will be "disengaged" by the time they are 29.[4]

To say that an overhaul of the public educational system is overdue is a huge understatement. I remember years ago hearing on the radio a description of the test that required a passing score in order to move on to high school from the eighth grade in the 1890s. Students were asked questions requiring a thorough knowledge of ancient history, classical literature, algebraic mathematics, Latin, and more. I was stunned when I realized I wouldn't have stood a chance of being promoted to high school with the "education" I received in our current educational system.

More recently, I heard an interview on YouTube where the "on the street" interviewer was asking university students some basic questions regarding relatively recent historical events. When the interviewer asked a female student who were the main combatants in World War II, after a few uhs and ums, it was obvious that the student didn't know the answer. I was astounded. It's hard to believe that having been alive for twenty years in the United States of America, one of the main combatants in World War II, chiefly responsible for defeating Germany, Italy, and Japan, and ostensibly saving the world from global tyranny, that an undergraduate could have somehow avoided stumbling onto that fact somewhere along the line.

Indeed, our public schools need an overhaul, and the stranglehold that teachers' unions and political PACs have had on the beliefs, philosophies, and practices in our schools needs to be relinquished and repudiated.

SO WHAT ARE OUR KIDS LEARNING?

To say that those steering the ship of public education are substituting wholesome, challenging, and intelligent curricula for "Doctrines of Demons" is not an exaggeration. This warning from apostle Paul to his disciple Timothy immediately comes to mind: "Now the Spirit expressly says that in latter times some will depart from the faith, giving heed to deceiving spirits and doctrines of demons" (1 Timothy 4:1).

The Marxist and secularist philosophies infiltrating

CHAPTER 5: OF THE CHILDREN

every level of education in America are purposefully devoid of God. They have been used for several decades now to reshape the foundational beliefs by which our country has historically operated. In essence, it is a plan to take over America from within, no shots fired.

The planned animus between different groups of people is the number-one strategy out of the Marxist playbook. You define an oppressor class and an oppressed class. In the case of the original Marxist ideology, the classes were the "haves and the have-nots," based on economic disparities. This fostered the Russian Revolution, which, of course, empowered those representing the oppressed class. The result was the creation of a third class not previously mentioned or possibly not even foreseen by those proponents of Marxism, a "New Ruling Class." In this case, the New Ruling Class, members of the Communist Party, then proceeded to distribute poverty equally amongst the masses while they lived in relative luxury. Sound familiar? Ironic that the Russian Revolution was fought to remove the monarchy, the "ruling elite," only to end up with a different group of despots! Lord Acton's axiom "Power corrupts. Absolute power corrupts absolutely" holds true like never before. Add to that the fact that when those who rule do so with no sense of responsibility before God and are committed to serving their ideological beliefs and not the interests of the people, tyranny is the inevitable result.

Fast forward to current times and we have various groups substituting race for economic disparity. The flagship of this ideology is called "critical race theory" (CRT).

CRT makes it sound like there's something critical that we need to learn about race that, until recently, we had not been aware of. I recently heard a black pastor give this explanation about race—and I'm paraphrasing here: "By the way, there is only one race when referring to people, the human race. The differentiation in color is merely a matter of how much melanin one is genetically disposed to produce." We are genetically and physiologically of the same "kind." Nevertheless, those advocating for such specious paradigms and philosophies as CRT are relentless in promoting division based on "race" as defined by skin color. This is the state of accepted belief we find in much of modern-day America.

Here is a brief description of one of the tenets of CRT from *Encyclopedia Britannica*:

THE SOCIAL CONSTRUCTION OF RACE AND THE NORMALITY OF RACISM

First, race is socially constructed, not biologically natural. The biogenetic notion of race—the idea that the human species is divided into distinct groups on the basis of inherited physical and behavioral differences—was finally refuted by genetic studies in the late 20th century. Social scientists, historians, and other scholars now agree that the notion of race is a social construction (though there is no consensus regarding what exactly a social construction is or what the process of social construction consists of). Some CRT theorists hold that race is an

CHAPTER 5: OF THE CHILDREN

artificial association or correlation between a set of physical characteristics—including skin colour, certain facial features, and hair texture—and an imagined set of psychological and behavioral tendencies, conceived as either positive or negative, good or bad. The associations have been created and maintained by dominant groups (in the United States, whites of Western European descent) to justify their oppression and exploitation of other groups on the basis of the latter's supposed inferiority, immorality, or incapacity for self-rule.[5]

The last sentence is laced with huge assumptions and stereotyping. It lumps together all those of Caucasian heritage as "justifying their oppression and exploitation of other groups on the basis of the latter's supposed inferiority, immorality, or incapacity for self-rule." I never knew that I was justifying the oppression and exploitation of other groups, did you? But this, CRT proponents claim, just further serves to prove that "white people" are unaware and/or ignorant of their inherent racism. Talk about the kettle calling the pot black, no racial pun intended. Aren't these generalizations about all "white people" nothing more than racist assumptions in and of themselves? And, again, the rebuttal to this by CRT promoters is that the very fact you may disagree with their claims regarding your "inherent racism" is to them evidence that you are blind to the fact that you possess it! This type of convoluted ideology is widely taught in public and private education.

Imagine you are a ten-year-old white student and your teacher just finished pontificating on the "truths" contained in CRT; she has just typecast you as an oppressor of some of your fellow students. Can you feel the daggers from your non-white classmates pointed in your direction? Not only are these CRT tenets little more than opinions rather than truths but they are purposefully divisive and promote reverse discrimination and racism, the very things they claim to be fighting against.

The lack of economic opportunities for people of color in modern-day America is a hard sell. Vision, purpose, and perseverance still pay high dividends to all who wish to employ them, regardless of skin color. So the focus has been shifted from mere economic inequality to "racial inequality," creating extended oppressed and oppressor groups in lockstep with standard Marxist operating procedure.

A fairly well-known interview with Don Lemon of CNN and Morgan Freeman, both African-Americans, was recorded on June 3, 2014. At one point Lemon asks Freeman, "Do you think that race plays a part in wealth distribution?" Freeman answers, "Today? No, I don't. You and I, we're proof. Why would race have anything to do with it?"[6]

I do realize that many African Americans sincerely hold views that align with the tenets of CRT, believing them to be true. However, a growing number of African Americans are turning away from the Marxist party line, acknowledging that modern America has provided them unlimited opportunities. There are, however, many people

CHAPTER 5: OF THE CHILDREN

of various colors that promote CRT as a means of obtaining political leverage as well as economic gain. The recent scandals of BLM receiving huge amounts of donation monies to further "the cause," only to see their leaders purchasing multiple properties and living extravagant lifestyles, support this assessment of the nefarious motives behind many in this movement.

The same can be said of other race-based ideologies, such as "The 1619 Project," which connects the founding of America to the arrival of the first slaves in the colonies rather than July 4, 1776, when the Declaration of Independence, the official and actual founding of the United States of America, was signed. Words fail to describe the many other philosophical notions that strive to replace the actual history of our country and which have been and are still being used to indoctrinate multiple generations into a perception of an America founded upon specious ideologies and not historical facts. Yet, these ideologies are widely taught and presented as undeniable truths, particularly in our public education systems.

Was there slavery in America? Yes, absolutely. Has there been serious racism in America? Yes, without a doubt. Are these awful practices dominating American society now? NO! The massive progress achieved in our societal and cultural beliefs and practices has moved us far away from these evils. Do racists still exist in America? Yes, but at a fractional percentage of the past. In fact, I have, in recent years, heard far more racial slurs coming from minorities directed at whites than the other way around. In my experience, I can't recall hearing a white person use the word "nigger" in at least fifty years, which takes me back to grade school when kids of every color had no aversion to engaging in racial name-calling. But as a nation, we have largely moved on, and that should be applauded and celebrated. What our children are taught in public and private education should reflect that. We need to disavow the odious notion that America is a nation completely plagued with systemic racism and promote once again that we are "One nation, under God, indivisible, with liberty and justice for all."

However, the above propaganda, veiled in pseudo-intellectual terms, is being widely taught in our public schools and universities. It is first anti-God, and it is also anti-American. The Founding Fathers repeatedly confirmed that the foundation of this nation is rooted in its acknowledgment of and dependence on the God revealed in the Holy Scriptures, the Bible. Sustaining liberty, they also contended, necessitated a religious and moral people to survive. This subject is further expanded upon in chapter 7, "The Fathers Knew Best."

SCHOOL LIBRARY OR ADULT BOOKSTORE?

Again, thanks to COVID-19, parents became shockingly aware that in many public-school libraries, and even in the classroom, highly sexually explicit and blatantly pornographic materials are readily available to students of all ages. Consider the following article:

CHAPTER 5: OF THE CHILDREN

"PROMOTING PORN IN SCHOOL LIBRARIES IS THE REAL PROBLEM, NOT 'BANNED BOOKS'"

In response to parents objecting to the state-sponsored sexualization of our children in public schools, the American Library Association (ALA) is hosting "Banned Books Week" from Oct. 1-7. The event is likely meant to distract Americans from an unfortunate reality: The taxpayer-funded ALA is trying to place pornographic books in the hands of children, while it tries to ban books and story hours with patriotic themes.

Few are soon to forget story hour with Sen. John Kennedy, R-La. On Sept 12, 2023, during the Senate Judiciary Committee hearing titled "Book Bans: Examining How Censorship Limits Liberty and Literature," Kennedy read excerpts from books currently in middle-school libraries across the country. From the pornographic book containing graphic pictures *Gender Queer*, the seventy-one-year-old read . . . (the actual description of the sexual acts has been left out due to the deviant and graphic nature of the text).

The article continues:

Kennedy's display made an incisive point: Books like *Gender Queer* and *All Boys Aren't Blue* meet the legal definition of pornography, and they do not belong in K-12 public school libraries. Even Maia Kobabe, the author of *Gender Queer*, agrees. She said, "I don't recommend this book for kids."

Others feel that 11-year-olds in middle school need access to these books to feel seen. Sen. Dick Durbin, D-Ill., for example, stated, "Every student deserves access to books that reflect their experiences and help them better understand who they are." It is unclear the children to whom the senator is referring, but if these passages reflect their experiences, they are victims in need of serious help.[7]

So how did we get to this point where those working in the educational system have become so emboldened to promote such deceptive philosophies and ideologies, while at the same time successfully expunging God and religion from public education? It has primarily happened as a result of a misapplication of the establishment clause in the First Amendment of the Constitution. It says:

Congress shall make no law respecting an establishment of religion, or prohibiting the free exercise thereof; or abridging the freedom of speech, or of the press; or the right of the people peaceably to assemble, and to petition the Government for a redress of grievances.

The phrase "a wall of separation between church and state" is derived from Thomas Jefferson's letter of January 1, 1802, to the Danbury Baptist Association, who had no intention of denying religious expression in public schools. Rather, the letter is written to staunchly reinforce the Constitutional protection of the citizen's right to practice

CHAPTER 5: OF THE CHILDREN

their religion free of governmental interference. I'm sure it would be a surprise to many who recite this phrase, claiming it to be Constitutional in order to justify their actions of censoring students' religious freedoms, to find out that it's not even in the Constitution!

The "Establishment Clause" was clearly intended to prevent what had been established in England, as well as in other European nations, from happening in the United States. The Church of England was established by the Crown as the official state religion. The ensuing corruption in the established church and persecution of any other religious denomination is what the Founding Fathers wished to prevent. Those championing the complete "separation of church and state" have presumed that this empowers them to prohibit any expression of religion in the classroom or school grounds as a whole. The stated purpose of this clause has been twisted and turned to grant any number of governing entities the power to legislate the prohibition of the "free exercise thereof." Whether done willfully or simply out of ignorance, it is utterly unconstitutional. A parallel in scripture can be seen in Peter's second epistle when he addresses those attempting to redefine scriptures, "which untaught and unstable people twist to their own destruction, as they do also the rest of the Scriptures" (2 Peter 3:16).

The slow and steady move away from biblical values and morality in public schools has coincided with the exponential rise in criminal actions, violence against teachers and other students, teen pregnancies, homosexual behavior, and the latest trend toward ungodliness, transgenderism. And, if you are truly concerned about a "pandemic," consider the explosion of sexually transmitted diseases since the mid-1960s, including the deadliest form, AIDS.

This excerpt is from the National Library of Medicine's article entitled "Sexually transmitted diseases in the USA: temporal trends":

> In general, data on reported STDs in the USA showed steady increases during the 1960s, with a leveling off or decline of most of the bacterial STDs but continual increases in viral STDs and genital chlamydial infections during the 1970s and 1980s. National reports of gonorrhea and syphilis began declining at different times and at different rates in all industrialized countries during the late 1980s and 1990s. However, since the turn of the century, a number of these declining trends have reversed.[8]

However, the situation is not hopeless. Parents across the country have become very active in confronting their local school boards and demanding a return to the three RRRs, Reading, Riting, and Rithmetic. In many cases, school-board members have been recalled or voted out of office. In one instance the entire board was recalled and replaced by concerned parents.

Last year parents in San Francisco, of all places, successfully recalled three school-board members due to their support of highly controversial curricula as previously

CHAPTER 5: OF THE CHILDREN

described, to be included in the K-12 public schools. If it can happen in San Francisco, a city not at all known for promoting conservative values, it can happen anywhere in the country.

However, the devastating effects of this carefully planned and executed departure from traditional educational methods, philosophies, and biblical morality cannot be underestimated. In case you were not aware, one of the textbooks first used when public education was established in the United States was the Bible. Now, we're seeing children derided for believing the Bible, and even forbidden and suspended for bringing their bible to school. This type of discrimination and outright persecution blatantly violates the highest law of the land, the United States Constitution. Various legal advocates for protecting the rights of citizens have had almost unanimous victory in holding teachers, administrators, and education officials accountable for such egregious violations of their students' Constitutional rights.

It's instructive to see the many videos, available online, that show what happens when parents have confronted school boards around the country. Let's just call the responses from school-board members "interesting." I have watched many videos of parents bringing to the attention of these board members that their public-school libraries contain highly inappropriate and even pornographic reading materials that are available, in some instances, to children of all ages.

To demonstrate the immoral and deviant nature of

the books, parents have read excerpts aloud in the school-board meetings and are often told in the context of the meeting that such reading material is "inappropriate." Ironic that many of these same school-board members will then not vote to have these books removed from the school libraries. The hypocrisy is obvious. You can't make this stuff up!

It is encouraging that many teachers, administrators, and board members are making it known that they do not agree with these controversial ideologies being taught, and call attention to the inappropriate materials circulating in public schools. They do this even at the risk of being reprimanded for their views and risk the possibility of losing their jobs. The tyrannical demands of the extreme left, on all who work in or are related to the public education system, must be stopped if we are to prevent another generation of our children being subject to this purposeful indoctrination into Marxist, humanist, and godless "education."

In California, where I reside, the legislature recently passed a bill that would threaten parents with possible removal of children from their homes if they talked to their children, who may be entertaining transgenderism, about why that is not the way to go. The state in its near-lunatic reasoning (I'm being kind here) argues that it considers anything other than affirming the child's imaginings about what gender they might wish to be as child abuse and dangerous to the child's emotional well-being. Truly the wisdom of men is foolishness before the Lord.

CHAPTER 5: OF THE CHILDREN

Our children have, for decades now, become the target of those determined to promote a godless agenda in our educational systems. They are relentlessly pursuing a path to complete their goal of "Cancel Culture," employing a long-term strategy to accomplish this by capturing the minds of our children. They are in "good" company. Vladimir Lenin, a founding leader of the communist regime of the Soviet Union, once proclaimed, "Give me four years to teach the children and the seed I have sown will never be uprooted."9

Shouldn't we rather be engaged in seeing to it that these evil seeds are never planted in the first place?

CHAPTER 6
GENDER CONDITIONING

Sexual indoctrination is being forced upon American children at an alarming rate. This "curriculum" has been injected with such speed that most parents had no idea these subjects were being taught to their children. And to listen to the media, both broadcast and social, one gets the impression that these radical and unbiblical ideas have been the norm all along.

Consider these viewpoints:

"Gender dysphoria" is the condition of "distress a person experiences due to a mismatch between their gender identity—their personal sense of their own gender—and their sex assigned at birth."[1]

Transgenderism seeks to normalize and even codify beliefs and behaviors that are at best delusional and more to the point symptomatic of mental illness. Advocates of transgenderism cannot appeal to any scientific verification that gender is fluid or is simply a matter of an emotional disposition. Every one of the approximately

CHAPTER 6: GENDER CONDITIONING

30 trillion cells in a person's body establishes their gender. The chromosome sets in a person's DNA is either XX for the female or XY for the male.[2]

The number of people who identify as transgender has doubled since 2017 until now, 2023, particularly among 13-24 year-olds.[3]

This seems to coincide with the rampant rush we have seen to flood school curricula with gender studies material, revealing a concerted effort by the departments of education at the local, state, and federal levels to inject these views from kindergarten through college. One might ask, who gave those in the educational system permission to start teaching these subjects that are neither scientifically affirmed and are completely without historical precedent, ever? Do they not know that no amount of surgery, hormonal treatment, or cultural indoctrination can alter the basic biological fact that the establishment of gender identity occurs at the genetic level, and as such is unalterable? "Professing to be wise, they became fools . . ." (Romans 1:22).

Here is an article in which the writer offers "helpful" suggestions to parents about their children who may consider themselves transgender. You have to ask yourself: would it even occur to a young child to ponder the ideology of transgenderism had it not been intentionally inserted into the school curriculum by school boards, administrators, and teachers?

"ACCEPTING YOUR CHILD'S GENDER-DIVERSE IDENTITY"

Research suggests that gender is something we are born with; it can't be changed by any interventions. It is critically important that children feel loved and accepted for who they are.

When disclosing their gender-diverse identity, some kids might expect immediate acceptance and understanding. However, there is evidence that family members go through their own process of becoming more comfortable and understanding of a child's gender identity, thoughts and feelings. One model suggests the process resembles the stages of grief: shock, denial, anger, bargaining and acceptance.

Just as gender-diverse children do best when their feelings are explored and validated, some parents may need their own emotional supports. They may also have many questions along their child's journey.

WHAT PARENTS CAN DO

When your child discloses their identity to you, respond in an affirming, supportive way. Understand that, although gender identity is not able to be changed, it often is revealed over time as people discover more about themselves.

Connect your child with LGBTQ organizations, resources and events. It is important for them to know they are not alone.[4]

CHAPTER 6: GENDER CONDITIONING

I was struck by the first sentence in the article; "Research confirms that gender is something we're born with; it can't be changed by any interventions." Since there is no scientific separation between sex and gender, the writer seemingly and unknowingly debunks his whole assertion that gender can be fluid or is simply a matter of mental assertion.

If the writer means "interventions" such as the necessity of ongoing hormonal injections and questionable, even dangerous, surgical procedures, I completely agree. I wonder if the writer realized what he was actually saying. Any lucid person would take that to mean that whatever sex you were born with, that is your gender, which cannot be changed.

This transgender advocate is definitely of the opinion that biological sex and gender are two separate things. Your sex cannot be changed, regardless of the medical gymnastics you may subject your body to, but this transgender advocate believes gender is separate and fluid, a matter of how a person feels about or imagines their gender to be.

Let's see what the Bible says. In Jeremiah 17:9, we are told, "The heart is deceitful above all things and desperately wicked, who can know it?"

The writer of the article has bought into the deception that gender is a state of mind, that it is what one chooses to believe they are and not what they are in reality. Also, notice that the writer claims gender is assigned at birth. Again, this is scientifically wrong; gender is determined at conception. As stated in the opening articles of this chapter, gender is synonymous with sex, and no amount of surgery and/or hormonal manipulation can change the genetic reality of gender that is present in every one of the approximately 30 trillion cells in the human body. "For You formed my inward parts; You wove me in my mother's womb. I will praise You, for I am fearfully and wonderfully made" (Psalm 139:13-14).

Gender is not alterable due to a changeable state of mind, and it is certainly not merely a personal choice. It is a biological fact. Do you think any reputable psychologist or psychiatrist would describe schizophrenia, obsessive compulsive disorder, or any number of delusional psychological disorders as conditions that should be treated as normal based on what the individual chooses to believe is true about themselves, and that these conditions must be responded to with acceptance and affirmation? They might, at the risk of losing their license to practice.

Nevertheless, LGBTQ advocates have done everything they can to fast-track this godless ideology into American culture in general and into our educational systems specifically. So what has been happening to more than a few of our minor children as a result of these pernicious ideologies?

First, I'm always astounded by the sheer presumption of those directing curriculum decisions in our public education system, along with the endorsement of numerous elected officials. They feel they have the purview to inject any type of teaching material into that system, regardless

CHAPTER 6: GENDER CONDITIONING

of how inappropriate and controversial it may be and with little or no regard for the desires, wishes, and beliefs of the parents. It has gotten so insane that recently parents who had the audacity to call school-board members across the country on the carpet for allowing such wretched material into the classrooms and libraries were actually labeled by the National School Boards Association as possibly being "Domestic Terrorists!" Attorney General Merrick Garland tasked the FBI with investigating this "imminent threat" to national security.[5] This is a lawless and complete misuse of authority and reveals the overarching agenda of the rabid ideologues in "public service," who serve a godless, and immoral, belief system bent on turning America into an anarchist bottomless pit, where anything goes except serving a "religious and moral people" as the Founding Fathers declared was necessary for the survival of a free Republic.

A quick aside here. The term "public servant" seems to have become almost laughable when applied to many in governmental positions who seem to view their role as that of a ruler and would sneer at the idea that they are employed at the behest of the people, and are, in fact, our servants. In the United States of America, serving the citizens is the true role of those in government and not the other way around.

Back to what has been happening to our children on the transgender front. Minors, and when I say minors, I'm including very young children who are encouraged to express their "gender preference" within the school system, have had hormonal treatments made available to them and have even been given access to surgical procedures often without parental notification. Again, who do these people think they are to presume they have the right and authority to assist in altering the life of a young person, who has neither the maturity, mentally or physically, nor the ability to comprehend the numerous lifelong consequences of such severe actions? Never mind that the whole idea of being able to truly change one's gender is a biological impossibility in the first place. Nonetheless, many in the school system have come to believe that "for the emotional health of the child," parents need not be informed of such life-altering decisions, especially if it is known by the "educators" that the parents would not consent to such radical procedures. Even if misguided parents would agree to subject their children to such dangerous interventions, the children should be legally protected from having to suffer the permanent consequences of specious medical procedures. I consider subjecting children to these often permanent, life-changing procedures one of the worst forms of child abuse and endangerment.

Here are some excerpts from an article on the NHS UK (National Health Service, United Kingdom) website regarding the effects of transgender treatments, primarily for minors.

CHAPTER 6: GENDER CONDITIONING

"PUBERTY BLOCKERS AND CROSS-SEX HORMONES"

Puberty blockers (gonadotrophin-releasing hormone analogues) pause the physical changes of puberty, such as breast development or facial hair.

Little is known about the long-term side effects of hormone or puberty blockers in children with gender dysphoria.

From the age of 16, teenagers who've been on hormone blockers for at least 12 months may be given cross-sex hormones, also known as gender-affirming hormones.

These hormones cause some irreversible changes, such as:

breast development (caused by taking oestrogen)
breaking or deepening of the voice (caused by taking testosterone)

Long-term cross-sex hormone treatment may cause temporary or even permanent infertility.

There is some uncertainty about the risks of long-term cross-sex hormone treatment.

RISKS OF HORMONE THERAPY

The most common risks or side effects include:

blood clots
gallstones
weight gain

acne
dyslipidaemia (abnormal levels of fat in the blood)
elevated liver enzymes
polycythemia (high concentration of red blood cells)
hair loss or balding (androgenic alopecia)

The aim of hormone therapy is to make you more comfortable with yourself, both in terms of physical appearance and how you feel. The hormones usually need to be taken for the rest of your life, even if you have gender surgery.[6]

If it takes such risky treatments to increase my level of comfort, count me out. What is the takeaway here? Is it not that these "gender-affirming hormones" are unnatural treatments? The body will not continue to produce these unnatural hormones. This means, according to the article, you will have to have some of these treatments "for the rest of your life."

The article further states that some individuals, due to genetic factors, will experience traits "that cannot be overcome simply by adjusting the dose." In other words, a person may retain either male or female characteristics despite the hormonal treatment they are receiving. So the possibility remains that a male who wishes to become a woman, physically and functionally, for example, could end up being something of a hybrid. Certainly not the outcome they wanted or would be comfortable with. What would be the frustrating emotional effects of this situation? Does it not further point to the non-viability of truly

CHAPTER 6: GENDER CONDITIONING

being able to change your gender? No matter what hormonal manipulation or surgical procedures you undergo, every chromosome in the body is hard-wired to replicate what it was created to be: male or female.

Again, what is trying to be achieved here is to treat a psychological disorder, not with therapy and counseling to overcome the disorder, but through chemical and surgical manipulations. The attempt is made to create a state of normalcy around the disorder. For the preponderance of history, the desire of a man to be a woman and vice versa was rightly deemed to be a mental condition that the individual had to come to terms with and embrace the reality of who they are or risk assignment to an asylum. It is only through the advent of medical technology that such an absurd idea of transitioning from one sex to the other could even be considered. Yet this is recklessly being accepted as a viable option for minors!

Now we get to the nitty-gritty of gender transition through surgical procedures. Take a look at what a person would have to go through to transition from one sex to the other. And remember, whatever a person subjects themselves to in the way of treatments, their genetics are never fooled. The NHS UK article continues:

Gender surgery for trans men includes:

"Common chest procedures for trans men (transmasculine people) include:

> removal of both breasts (bilateral mastectomy) and associated chest reconstruction

nipple repositioning
dermal implant and tattoo

Gender surgery for trans men includes:

construction of a penis (phalloplasty or metoidioplasty)
construction of a scrotum (scrotoplasty) and testicular implants
a penile implant
removal of the testes (orchidectomy)
removal of the penis (penectomy)
construction of a vagina (vaginoplasty)
construction of a vulva (vulvoplasty)
construction of a clitoris (clitoroplasty)
Removal of the womb (hysterectomy) and the ovaries and fallopian tubes (salpingo-ophorectomy) may also be considered.

Gender surgery for trans women includes:

Breast implants for trans women (trans-feminine people) are not routinely available on the NHS.
Facial feminization surgery and hair transplants are not routinely available on the NHS.
As with all surgical procedures, there can be complications. Your surgeon should discuss the risks and limitations of surgery with you before you consent to the procedure."

CHAPTER 6: GENDER CONDITIONING

After reading this frightening description of gender transition surgery, what immediately popped into my mind was Mary Shelley's famous novel *Frankenstein*. Although it sounds humorous, I'm not at all trying to be funny here. In the book, Dr. Frankenstein created something unnatural that was never meant to be. You can see the parallel. Humans, trying to play God, never seem able to fully achieve the desired outcome.

This is the gruesome reality we see being nonchalantly accepted by the general population and put into practice by the medical community. All of it displays a lack of belief in God and willful ignorance of the fact that there is a day of reckoning for every human who has ever or will ever live.

Undoubtedly many healthcare professionals are sincere in their belief that "transgenderism" is normal for some individuals and that they are helping fulfill a valid emotional and medical need. They are, however, sincerely wrong. As was, and still is the case with COVID-19, many in the medical field and related businesses are being incentivized by lucrative fees and a plethora of government subsidies for services and treatments provided.[7]

To illustrate this kind of monetary motivation, I remember when my wife Judy was pregnant with our second child, we made our appointment with the same doctor who delivered our first. He was, it had seemed, very family friendly and took great joy in delivering babies for his patients. He had a wall covered with photos of numerous happy and healthy babies that he had helped bring into the world, and he seemed to take great pride in that.

After the initial examination, and as we were preparing to leave, seemingly out of nowhere the doctor said, "So we don't have to take it away." It took a few seconds to grasp what he was actually saying. We were shocked by this statement. When we realized that he was willing to perform an abortion if we so desired, we told him that we could not agree to continue to have him as our doctor given that he performs abortions, something that was completely against our beliefs. We had not expressed any desire to terminate the pregnancy, so there is no reason for him to have brought this up in the first place. Perhaps the insurance coverage for a surgical procedure was more profitable than a normal delivery. Everything about his practice and his communications with us until that point reflected a sincere belief that he was all in on delivering the best care to the mother and child, as in participating in the miracle of the birth of a new human being.

At the time abortion had only recently been legalized, so for much of his practice, abortion was not even an option. It appears more and more within the medical profession that the tenet "Do no harm" has been reduced to a subjective ideal, often turned on its head through convoluted and godless reasoning. I'm sure that few medical professionals would admit it, but what may have been at play here is the age-old adage "money talks."

CHAPTER 6: GENDER CONDITIONING

INDOCTRINATION

Indoctrination within the educational system has been appearing in more and more public and private schools in recent years. This section could have been included in the previous chapter, "Of the Children," but I felt it was so relevant to the discussion on transgenderism that I decided to include it here. Here are some excerpts from an article published by the California Family Council entitled:

"PARENTS PUBLICLY EXPOSE SECRET ELEMENTARY LGBTQ CLUBS IN ELK GROVE"

> Parents at a California elementary school were alarmed in January after discovering a 3rd-grade teacher was allowed to personally invite all the 3rd through 6th-grade classes to a new LGBTQ club he was starting. The "UBU Club" aka. "you be you," as he called it, was for "boys who crush on boys" and "girls who crush on girls," but anyone could come, the kids were told. Yet parents weren't told anything about the club. No notification in the school newsletter and no permission slips were required for attendance, despite one being necessary to belong to the school's garden club.

Let's pause here for a moment. It is obvious that "standard operating procedure" at this school is that participation in any club the school sponsors requires not only parental notification but parental permission as well.

Incredible that parental permission to join something as innocuous as the Garden Club is required, yet participation in something as controversial and deviant for minor children as the LGBTQ club is not. The obvious takeaway here is that those promoting this "club" feel the need to engage in a devious tactic to establish it—i.e., keep it secret from the children's parents. Although they try to justify this clandestine approach by claiming they are concerned about the children's mental and emotional health, it instead reveals a desire to indoctrinate their students into woke agendas without having to risk parental backlash. Fortunately, in this case, that didn't go so well.

Now I'm not advocating the following course of action but to make a point of how much things have changed in the last sixty years. I can remember when I was a child in the early 1960s. If any adult, including teachers, and specifically in this case a male teacher, presumed to intrude into a child's and their family's lives by secretly inviting their child to join a club, of a sexual nature, without the parents' knowledge and, more importantly, their consent, most fathers would have invited that teacher to a private meeting out behind the "barn!"

There is an amazing level of presumption by so many in the educational field today, believing that they have a right to impose their ideology, regardless of what the beliefs and upbringing of other people's children are. For lack of a more eloquent description, this assumed liberty taken by those in the educational field is disturbing at best. Meanwhile, back to the article:

CHAPTER 6: GENDER CONDITIONING

Within days of finding out, 30 upset parents crowded into a meeting room with the principal of Elk Grove's Pleasant Grove Elementary School and a district administrator to get some answers. They were told LGBTQ clubs had already been started in 5 to 10 other elementary schools. They also discovered school officials weren't sure students needed parent permission to attend an LGBTQ club. But the UBU club was put on hold until the school officials got legal advice.[8]

It's good that the club was put on hold. But notice the club wasn't put on hold because the school officials had any regard for the parents' concerns; they put it on hold until they determined if they were in any legal jeopardy before authorizing the club's establishment. Once again, here are "public servants" acting with our best interests at heart. Sarcasm intended.

These types of occurrences illustrate just how convoluted moral thinking has become in our culture in general and in our educational system specifically. It was admirable that the parents took action in confronting the school board due to the lack of parental notice and permission before the launching of this club. However, my question to the school board would not have been why notification and permission were not sought but why was such a "club," which would certainly have been viewed by many parents as inappropriate in an elementary school, be given serious consideration in the first place? I would have gone further and brought into question whether the teacher advocating for such a gathering of minor students, who physiologically are not even able to engage in sexual activity, should not be severely disciplined for pursuing such a course of action if not outright terminated for his obvious lack of moral character and sound judgment.

At the moment there seems to be very little protection in the form of political and/or legal resolve standing between these specious and godless ideologies that are flooding our schools. Thank God there is a bright ray of hope as an increasing number of parents and grandparents are standing up and joining the fight! There is no question where right and wrong lie in this matter. The wrong, in this case, needs only "good people to do nothing" to realize their ultimate victory in decimating all godly morality and institutionalizing their desire for a secularist, humanistic, and atheistic society. If successful, they, along with us, will suffer an unintended result: rampant lawlessness, an ever-increasing and oppressive government implementing ever-increasing and oppressive legislation, and an increasing decline in every sphere of our society. An even more ominous result has been that America's enemies have not failed to take notice either. Our growing weakness has only served to embolden them in their quest for world domination, which increases tensions and the fearful specter of global conflict.

Let us hold our ground with these words: "Righteousness exalts a nation, but sin is a reproach to any people" (Proverbs 14:34).

CHAPTER 7
THE FATHERS KNEW BEST

One of the most important figures in the history of this country is Robert Hunt. Although not considered one of the Founding Fathers in the common and historical sense, he nonetheless was one whose actions were truly foundational in the establishment of America as "One nation under God." On April 9, 1607, what I consider the most important and binding act that was ever performed in this country occurred at Cape Henry, Virginia. Upon coming ashore, a seven-foot roughly hewn wooden cross was planted in the sand, and Robert Hunt proceeded to make the following declaration:

> We do hereby dedicate this Land, and ourselves, to reach the People within these shores with the Gospel, to raise up Godly generations after us, and with these generations take the Kingdom of God to all the earth. May this Covenant of Dedication remain to all generations, as long as this earth remains, and may this Land, along with England, be Evangelist to the World. May all who see this Cross, remember

what we have done here, and may those who come here to inhabit join us in this Covenant and in this most noble work that the Holy Scriptures may be fulfilled.[1]

Throughout much of our history, and certainly in the current culture of our country, this declaration and covenant has either been largely unknown and/or purposefully ignored. Most in the America of today would not accept this covenant as relevant or in any way binding upon us. But none of us was there and therefore have nothing to say about whether or not it is binding on all who were born here or who have immigrated to this country. Few of us in modern America left all that we knew and had behind, risking our lives to begin a new life in a new land. Certainly, none of us made that perilous journey across the ocean, so none of us has any say as to the efficacy of the declaration. All of us, however, have been the beneficiaries of a nation "whose God is the Lord," though few of us today truly appreciate that this incalculable blessing was indeed bestowed upon us by God. And God, whether we choose to be bound by this dedication of America to Him or not, still holds America to the terms of this covenant. If you have any knowledge of the Bible, you know that God takes covenants very seriously.

Moving ahead 169 years to the signing of the Declaration of Independence, and subsequently the ratification of the United States Constitution, we find the same beliefs and devotion to God as the overriding principles upon which these documents and this nation were founded.

CHAPTER 7: THE FATHERS KNEW BEST

CHRISTIAN BELIEFS AND VALUES

The following quotes from some of the most prominent of the Founding Fathers lay to rest modern-day assertions by those quite removed from the events that America was not founded upon biblical Christian values and precepts:

> I've lived, sir, a long time, and the longer I live, the more convincing proofs I see of this truth—that God governs in the affairs of men. –Benjamin Franklin

> My views ... are the result of a life of inquiry and reflection, very different from the anti-Christian system imputed to me by those who know nothing of my opinions. To the corruptions of Christianity I am, indeed, opposed; but not to the genuine precepts of Jesus himself. I am a Christian in the only sense in which he wished anyone to be; sincerely attached to his doctrines in preference to all others. –Thomas Jefferson

> One great advantage of the Christian religion is that it brings the great principle of the law of nature and nations, love your neighbor as yourself, and do unto others as you would that others should do unto you, to the knowledge, belief, and veneration of the whole people. –John Adams

> Whilst we assert for ourselves a freedom to embrace, to profess, and to observe the religion we believe to be of

divine origin, we cannot deny an equal freedom to those whose minds have not yet yielded to the evidence that has convinced us. If this freedom be abused, it is an offense against God, not against man: To God, therefore, not to man, must an account of it be rendered. —James Madison

I have thought proper to recommend, and I hereby recommend accordingly, that Thursday the twenty-fifth day of April next, be observed throughout the United States of America as a day of solemn humiliation, fasting, and prayer; that the citizens ... call to mind our numerous offenses against the most high God, confess them before Him with the sincerest pertinence, implore His pardoning mercy, and through the great Mediator and Redeemer ... and that through the grace of the Holy Spirit, we may be disposed and enabled to yield a more suitable obedience to His righteous requisitions in time to come; ... that He would make us deeply sensible that "righteousness exalteth a nation but sin is a reproach to any people" (Proverbs 14:34). —John Adams[2]

Many in academia today wish to deny that the overarching belief system and worldview of the Founding Fathers of America were primarily Christian and necessarily biblical but are rather proponents of some form of deism at best. This view is embraced not because of a lack of historical evidence of Christian values and beliefs but by a secularist paradigm desperately grasping at straws to convince the citizenry that our founding was based on

CHAPTER 7: THE FATHERS KNEW BEST

something other than what it was, biblical Christian values. It always seems amazing to me how, the farther away from the actual events of history we get, the greater the liberty taken in interpreting those events when neither the philosophical understanding nor cultural context of the times seems to be given serious weight and consideration.

Consider the phrase "separation of church and state" that has, in modern times, been used to justify restriction and outright removal of even the mention of religion in public institutions. As previously mentioned to the surprise of many, even many Christians, this phrase does not appear in the Constitution but rather is taken from a letter written by Thomas Jefferson to the Danbury Baptist Association on January 1, 1802.

Here is an excerpt from that letter:

Mr. President
To messers Nehemiah Dodge, Ephraim Robbins, & Stephen S. Nelson, a committee of the Danbury Baptist Association in the state of Connecticut.
Gentlemen,
The affectionate sentiments of esteem and approbation which you are so good as to express towards me, on behalf of the Danbury Baptist association, give me the highest satisfaction. My duties dictate a faithful and zealous pursuit of the interests of my constituents, & in proportion as they are persuaded of my fidelity to those duties, the discharge of them becomes more and more pleasing.

Believing with you that religion is a matter which lies solely between Man & his God, that he owes account to none other for his faith or his worship, that the legitimate powers of government reach actions only, & not opinions, I contemplate with sovereign reverence that act of the whole American people which declared that their legislature should "make no law respecting an establishment of religion, or prohibiting the free exercise thereof," thus building a wall of separation between Church & State. [Congress thus inhibited from acts respecting religion, and the Executive authorized only to execute their acts, I have refrained from prescribing even those occasional performances of devotion, practiced indeed by the Executive of another nation as the legal head of its church, but subject here, as religious exercises only to the voluntary regulations and discipline of each respective sect.] Adhering to this expression of the supreme will of the nation in behalf of the rights of conscience, I shall see with sincere satisfaction the progress of those sentiments which tend to restore to man all his natural rights, convinced he has no natural right in opposition to his social duties.

I reciprocate your kind prayers for the protection & blessing of the common father and creator of man, and tender you for yourselves and your religious association assurances of my high respect & esteem.

(signed)

Thomas Jefferson, Jan.1.1802.[3]

CHAPTER 7: THE FATHERS KNEW BEST

The phrase "wall of separation between Church and State" was clearly stated by Jefferson to address the issue of a government, state or federal, mandating a specific religion as the only legal and authorized religion. Notice that you rarely, if ever, hear the second half of the establishment clause, "or prohibiting the free practice thereof" recited by those usurping its meaning for their own purposes.

There are endless examples of governmental bodies, particularly in education, which routinely engage in prohibiting the free exercise of religion and free speech. And what justification do they use to defend their actions? They claim to be acting in accordance with the Constitutional requirement of maintaining the "separation of church and state." Most who employ this justification for their actions are usually ignorant of the fact, whether willfully or not, that the phrase "wall of separation between church and state" isn't in the Constitution.

Jefferson was a staunch supporter of the free exercise of religion. His clear conviction was that the government had to be kept from interfering with and/or mandating a particular religious sect, and not that people's religious freedom and expression could be infringed upon by the government.

If the words of the Founding Fathers are considered in total and taken in the context of the culture of the day, it should not be hard then to come to a consensus as to the values by which they chose to constitute this nation. Let's look at the statements of belief of some of the most influential founders in America's formation.

Consideration of the Founding Fathers' religious beliefs must certainly begin with those of George Washington, the father of our nation. These are excerpts from two of Washington's prayers:

Sunday Evening Prayer:

O most Glorious God, in Jesus Christ my merciful and loving Father, I acknowledge and confess my guilt ... Let me live according to those holy rules which Thou hast this day prescribed in Thy holy word ... increase my faith, and direct me to the true object, Jesus Christ the Way, the Truth and the Life. These weak petitions, I humbly implore Thee to hear, accept and answer for the sake of Thy dear Son, Jesus Christ our Lord, Amen.

A Prayer for Wednesday Morning:

Almighty and Eternal Lord God, the Creator of Heaven and Earth, and the God and Father of our Lord Jesus Christ ... forgive my enemies, take me unto Thy protection this day, keep me in perfect peace, which I ask in the name and for the sake of Jesus. Amen.[4]

Washington's prayers are laced with biblical references, leaving no doubt as to the source of and the object of his belief. His faith was undeniably rooted in the God of the scriptures, the Bible, and his salvation through his belief in the finished work of Jesus Christ.

Regarding Washington's belief in Divine Providence

CHAPTER 7: THE FATHERS KNEW BEST

and the necessity of Almighty God's protection, consider the following excerpts:
Divine Providence and Protection:

> It is the duty of all Nations to acknowledge the providence of Almighty God, to obey His will, to be grateful for His benefits, and humbly to implore His Protection and favor.[5]

> ... by the miraculous care of Providence, that protected me beyond all human expectation; I had four bullets through my coat, and two horses shot under me, and yet escaped unhurt.[6]

Next, we will consider perhaps the greatest statesman America has ever produced. Printer, philosopher, scientist, honored intellectual, diplomat to England and France, signer of the Declaration of Independence and the Constitution, founder of the University of Pennsylvania, and considered the most respected man in the colonies, Benjamin Franklin.[7]

In the final debate of the Constitutional Convention held on June 28, 1787, the delegates were at an impasse related to representation and voting. It was at this point the eighty-one-year-old statesman stood to address the delegates and the president, George Washington.

Franklin's address:

> Mr. President,
> The small progress we have made after four or five weeks close attendance & continual reasonings with

each other—our different sentiments on almost every question, several of the last producing as many noes as ays, is me thinks a melancholy proof of the imperfection of human understanding. . . . In this situation of this assembly, groping as it were in the dark to find political truth, and scarce able to distinguish it when presented to us, how has it happened, Sir, that we have not hitherto once thought of humbly applying to the Father of Lights to illuminate our understanding! . . . I have lived, Sir, a long time, and the longer I live, the more convincing proofs I see of this truth—that God governs in the affairs of men. And if a sparrow cannot fall to the ground without His notice, is it probable that an empire can rise without His aid? We have been assured, Sir, in the sacred writings, that "except the Lord build the house, they labor in vain that build it." I firmly believe that without His concurring aid, we shall succeed in this political building no better than the builders of Babel. . . . I therefore beg leave to move—that henceforth prayers imploring the assistance of Heaven, and its blessings on our deliberations, be held in this assembly every morning before we proceed to business, and that one or more of the clergy of this city be requested to officiate in that service.[8]

Franklin's address, as was the case with Washington's prayers, makes several references to scripture. Naysayers have claimed Franklin was a deist and therefore did not hold Christian beliefs. The latter address at the

CHAPTER 7: THE FATHERS KNEW BEST

Constitutional Convention, as well as many of his writings, proves otherwise. Facts are stubborn things.

If there remains any question as to where Franklin's beliefs and faith are derived, here is Franklin's paraphrasing of the Lord's Prayer, first recorded in the Book of Matthew 6:9-13.

> Heavenly Father, may all revere Thee, and become Thy dutiful children and faithful subjects. May Thy Laws be obeyed on earth as perfectly as they are in Heaven. Provide for us this day as Thou hast hitherto daily done. Forgive us our trespasses, and enable us to likewise forgive those that offend us. Keep us out of temptation and deliver us from evil.[9]

Next, let's consider James Madison, a member of the Continental Congress, record keeper of the Constitutional Convention, author of twenty-nine of the Federalist papers, a member of the first United States Congress, author of the Bill of Rights, US Secretary of State, and fourth President of the United States.

Madison was highly educated in Latin, Greek, Spanish, French, mathematics, and literature. His tutors also established a comprehensive reading curriculum. He attended Princeton, initially studying for the ministry. He was strongly influenced by a leading theologian and scholar, the Reverend John Witherspoon. Madison became a champion defender of religious freedom. While serving in the first United States Congress, he wrote and advocated for

AMERICA: LOST AND FOUND

the Bill of Rights. The first item in the Bill of Rights is that of religious freedom.

Madison defined religion as follows:

> Religion, or the duty we owe to our Creator, and the manner of discharging it, can be directed only by reason and conviction, not by force or violence; and, therefore, that all men should enjoy the fullest toleration in the exercise of religion according to the dictates of conscience, unpunished and unrestrained by the magistrate, unless under the color of religion any man disturb the peace, the happiness, or the safety of society, and that it is the mutual duty of all to practice Christian forbearance, love, and charity towards each other.[10]

Again, we see a Founding Father of significant stature referencing the Bible and espousing Christian virtues in his writings as the guiding principles by which all the citizens of the Republic ought to observe and practice.

The litany of Christians among the Founding Fathers is extensive. The Christian faith, in particular, and a biblical worldview in general establishes an understanding of their overwhelming influence upon American society, the construction of its government, and the context and content of the Constitution of the United States. Truly, can it be said, "The Fathers Knew Best."

CHAPTER 8
EMBRACING THE FEAR OF THE LORD

I want to exit the highway we've been on and pull into a rest stop before we dive into the final chapters of this book. I have come to realize that the Fear of the Lord is the one posture that truly increases our love for and reverence of the Lord. Both are necessary components for the seeds of revival to grow. Hunger and thirst for God precipitate our capacity to receive the blessings promised by Jesus in His Sermon on the Mount, "Blessed are those who hunger and thirst for righteousness, For they shall be filled" (Matthew 5:6). As we set our hearts to search for a deeper relationship and revelation of the Lord in the Fear of God, it seems impossible not to have our first love rekindled and our passion for His purposes revitalized.

Have you struggled to wrap your mind around what it actually means to "Fear the Lord" and at the same time not be afraid of Him? I think we have all. It can seem that these two ideas are at odds with each other. However, I believe that the Fear of the Lord is the starting block of successful spiritual warfare. We need to have a healthy fear and awe of God as the operating platform in our spiritual paradigm. The stronger our belief in the unlimited power, unlimited genius, unlimited love, righteous judgment, complete faithfulness, and utter holiness of our God, the greater our trust and confidence that He truly is able to do "exceedingly abundantly above all that we ask or think, according to the power that works in us" (Ephesians 3:20).

Slogans like "Jesus is my co-pilot," while I appreciate the sentiment, highly diminish the actual nature of God. We should never view Him casually. The word says, "It is a fearful thing to fall into the hands of the living God" (Hebrews 10:31).

I chose to address the topic of the Fear of the Lord in this chapter because it has become clear that many of us in the Christian community have, at times, had a somewhat laissez-faire attitude regarding the gravitas of Almighty God. In the previous chapter, "The Fathers Knew Best," you'll notice how they always refer to the Lord in reverential terms and with complete respect and awe. When we are aware that we are experiencing the presence of the Lord, it is an awesome and wonderful experience! It is never to be taken lightly. When we do not operate in a healthy Fear of the Lord, it seems to become easier to bend or break the "rules." Once again, to clarify, I'm not talking about earning your salvation. That can only be obtained by God's grace, through faith in Jesus Christ, and not by anything we do to try and earn it. But the reality of the spiritual law

CHAPTER 8: EMBRACING THE FEAR OF THE LORD

of sowing and reaping has never, and will never, lose its force. We will reap whatever we sow.

In 1962 a comedy album called *The First Family* was produced. It was a very funny parody about the life of President John F. Kennedy, his family, and those in and around his administration. In one scene the president and some of his friends and family are playing football on the White House lawn. One of the players questioned some of the president's rules that he didn't agree with. President Kennedy responded by saying, "When you play with me, you play by my rules, or you don't play at all!" The man asked, "Why is that?" and the President responded, "Because it's my ball!"[1] This, of course, is a humorous way to point out who's in charge—but you get the drift.

So how much more serious should our attitude be toward the One who not only owns this earthly ball but created it in the first place? Should we not live in a sacred commitment to "walk in the Spirit and not in the flesh," to honor and obey the Lord? That, in a nutshell, is what having the Fear of the Lord should look like in every aspect of our lives. The scriptures below bear this out:

And whatever you do, do it heartily as to the Lord and not to men (Colossians 3:23).

Oh, fear the Lord, you His saints! There is no want to those who fear Him (Psalm 34:9).

The fear of the Lord is the beginning of wisdom (Psalm 111.10).

The fear of God is often a misunderstood topic. When we think of fear, it is usually in a negative context, something that is not of God and should therefore be avoided. In the case of the fear of man or the fear of the devil, a foreboding fear of what might happen in the future, then, yes, these are the kinds of fear that we should avoid. More than that, we should not even tolerate them in our lives. The Word says in I John 4:18, "There is no fear in love; but perfect love casts out fear, because fear involves torment. But he who fears has not been made perfect in love."

But when we are referring to the Fear of the Lord, we are talking about something altogether different. The Fear of the Lord means to hold a sacred reverence toward God and to embrace with all sincerity of conviction that His Word is true and binding. It means to possess a sober understanding that "God is not mocked; for whatever a man sows, that he will also reap." In case there is any doubt as to whom this scripture applies, the passage is from Galatians 6:7, which Paul wrote to believers.

It's true many scriptures tell us to "fear not," but there are also many that tell us to fear God. This is succinctly explained in this excerpt from John Bevere's amazing book, *The Awe of God*:

> Some folks will rightly remind us that the Bible tells us, about 365 times, to "fear not," and this leads many Christians to conclude that God does not want us to fear. But these verses refer to destructive fear. Additionally, I can point out almost 200 in the Bible that encourage us to "fear God." And here's the unfortunate part: in our

CHAPTER 8: EMBRACING THE FEAR OF THE LORD

quest to eliminate any fear in our lives (including the virtue of fearing God), this area of our faith has been left unexamined, untried, and without benefit. The fear of the Lord is more glorious, more awe-inspiring, and even more joyous than we could ever imagine.[2]

John once shared about a meeting he had with once-famous televangelist Jim Bakker while Jim was serving his prison sentence. John, upon concluding his meeting with Jim, said "he just had to know when he (Jim) stopped loving Jesus?" Jim replied, "You don't understand; I never stopped loving Jesus. I just stopped fearing Him."

Did you ever work for someone or had a teacher in your life who was a heavyweight in their field? They carried such respect in their field that you knew to choose your words wisely when you were around them. You knew if you made an off-hand comment or spoke unwisely, the response from such a person would reveal a level of insight and understanding that you did not possess and might be rather embarrassing as well. I think we would all agree that this was a healthy fear that kept us from suffering "foot-in-mouth" disease. Almost all analogies used to illustrate some parallel truth about the Lord break down in some aspect, but if we extend such a high level of respect to a fellow human being as described above, how much more magnified should our sense of respect, honor, and awe be toward Almighty God who holds our lives in His hand?

The scripture says: "Render therefore to all their due:

taxes to whom taxes are due, customs to whom customs, *fear to whom fear, honor to whom honor*" (Romans 13:7). Emphasis added.

This verse instructs us to extend fear and honor to people who are deserving of it. When applied to the Lord, the inference is obvious. The promises and benefits of maintaining a healthy fear of the Lord are numerous. I encourage the reader to do even a cursory search on "the Fear of the Lord." You may be surprised by what an awesome gift it is and why we are so often instructed to understand and embrace it. We are promised that "our days will be prolonged," "His secrets are with those who fear Him," "the Lord keeps His eye on those who fear Him." The Fear of the Lord will bring you deliverance, mercy, righteousness, and on your children's children: wisdom and understanding, the blessings of God, the knowledge of God, and strong confidence.

I'll stop here having only gotten through a portion of Proverbs. You'll have to do the rest of the searching for yourself. But this gives us a taste of the rich blessings and promises God bestows on those who fear Him. That the Fear of the Lord is good, and more than good, is never in doubt. It is necessary for us to receive and partake in the multitude of blessings that God promises.

The greater the understanding that we have of and the more we embrace the Fear of the Lord, the more our boldness will increase in representing Him and His gospel to individuals in our immediate sphere of influence and to the world corporately as His Ekklesia, that is, His body on

CHAPTER 8: EMBRACING THE FEAR OF THE LORD

earth. The more we know in our knowers how vast is the power and how magnificent the being of God is, the more we will be kept from fearing anything of a lesser nature.

"The fear of the Lord is clean, enduring forever" (Psalm 19:9).

CHAPTER 9
NOT OF THIS WORLD—PART 1

Congratulations on making it this far! We have arrived at what I consider the payoff point. I believe we are arriving at the desired outcome of this book: to be encouraged and inspired to reach for greater things, especially in the affairs of our nation. As the old US Army TV jingle used to say, "Be all that you can be, in the Army." To paraphrase it slightly, "Be all that God has called you to be in His army." So let's dive in.

In 1976 Christian theologian and philosopher, Francis Schaeffer wrote a wonderful book entitled; *How Should We Then Live?*[1] Schaeffer wrote about various ages in human history, focusing on the decline of cultures. Considering the decline of our own Christian culture in the West, how ought we to respond and how ought we to then live out our Christian faith?

The answer comes from Jesus:

CHAPTER 9: NOT OF THIS WORLD—PART 1

If you were of the world, the world would love its own. Yet because you are not of the world, but I chose you out of the world, therefore the world hates you (John 15:19).

John 15:19 can be a hard pill to swallow for many of us, even though we are sincere followers of Christ. After all we naturally, or perhaps unnaturally, want to be liked by others. It's no fun to be hated. But Jesus said this as a statement of fact, a prophetic word if you will. Personally, I have found it hard to embrace this fact. I know it is the truth because Jesus said it, but it really goes against the grain of my emotional desire to be "liked." After all, "I'm a good guy, aren't I?" Therein lies the catch. In my insecurity, I tend to place value on how others feel about me, desiring that they only have "good thoughts" toward me. I know this is wrong thinking, but if the "old man" is anything, he is fearful, without a sense of purpose, and hopelessly insecure. And how could he be otherwise? After all, true security comes only from knowing that you have been "accepted in the Beloved" (Ephesians 1:6), meaning, in Jesus. More than once, I have been disappointed because I put my hope of happiness in people and things. Be it family members, friends, bosses, professors, political leaders (God help us!), careers, cars, houses, boats.... The scripture describes this mindset.

Thus says the Lord: "Cursed is the man who trusts in man and makes flesh his strength, whose heart departs from the Lord" (Jeremiah 17:5).

Now, my heart has never truly departed from the Lord,

but I have found that there are times when I rested my hope in something other than the Lord.

I clearly remember a time over twenty years ago when I made the mental decision that I had to take control of my finances. I had always been very involved in serving the Lord, and I assumed that, because of that one aspect of my life, I would naturally prosper.

After many years of financial struggle, the prospering didn't seem to occur, I decided to take matters into my own hands. I got involved in multilevel marketing. Although there were a lot of Christians involved, the business, if I am completely honest, had a Spirit of Mammon attached to it. After achieving some initial success, I found that the high level of commitment required to truly succeed, both emotionally and in terms of time, was more than I was willing to invest. For me, my hope had been placed in a manmade business system. Now let me interject I believe that, for many people, involvement in this type of business is where the Lord has led them. However, it was not the Lord's leading for me. I left the business and began the long journey back to reestablishing once again that my hope was solely in the Lord. Whatever enterprise I was going to involve myself with had to be led and blessed by God. Lesson learned.

STAYING ON TASK

During the American Civil War, the leader of the Union forces was General George McClellan. He was loved by

CHAPTER 9: NOT OF THIS WORLD—PART 1

his men, and he loved them as well. He spent months in training mode; all the while the Confederate Army was making significant advances. On several occasions, President Lincoln expressed his desire for McClellan to engage the Confederate forces. General McClellan resisted moving prematurely to engage in battle because he felt his troops weren't adequately prepared to successfully fight the enemy. President Lincoln had finally had enough of McClellan's reticence to fight and replaced him with a general who possessed a street fighter mentality named Ulysses S. Grant. The rest is history!

I recount this story because I believe it has striking parallels to what the Body of Christ has and has not done over the last several decades. The great healing revivals of the 1950s saw many thousands of recorded and medically verified healings and outright miracles occurring along with tens of thousands of people coming to faith in Christ. In the 1960s the great Charismatic Renewal began in which the supernatural gifts of the Spirit were rediscovered and embraced by significant numbers of Christians. They rejected an entrenched dispensational theology characterized by an unbiblical belief that the gifts of the Spirit were no longer available to us today. In the 1970s the amazing Jesus People Movement saw millions of people in the US and worldwide come to faith in Jesus Christ. From the 1980s to the present, significant outpourings of the Spirit such as the Vineyard Movement, the Toronto Blessing, and the Brownsville Revival have occurred, as well as a great expansion of ministries around the world marked

AMERICA: LOST AND FOUND

by demonstrations of the Holy Spirit's power. Numerous documented miraculous healings including an increasing number of actual resurrections from the dead continue to occur. It is no surprise that it was recently reported that the number of people coming to faith in Jesus has surpassed the number of babies being born worldwide. That is amazing and wonderful news.

It seems that we "Jesus People" are accomplishing Mark 16:15-18:

> And He said to them, "Go into all the world and preach the gospel to every creature. He who believes and is baptized will be saved; but he who does not believe will be condemned. And these signs will follow those who believe: In My name they will cast out demons; they will speak with new tongues; they will take up serpents; and if they drink anything deadly, it will by no means hurt them; they will lay hands on the sick, and they will recover."

All this should be celebrated, giving God great Glory for what He has done in most of our lifetimes, and continues to do now. However, and there is a however, we find another commission in Matthew that we have only been partially successful in completing.

And Jesus came and spoke to them, saying:

> All authority has been given to Me in heaven and on earth. Go therefore and *make disciples of all the nations*, baptizing them in the name of the Father and of the Son and of

CHAPTER 9: NOT OF THIS WORLD—PART 1

the Holy Spirit, teaching them to observe all things that I have commanded you; and lo, I am with you always, even to the end of the age. Amen (Matthew 28:18-20). Emphasis added.

Now Jesus doesn't say, to make disciples *in* all the nations, which is how I had always taken it to mean; He says, "make disciples *of* all nations." The difference is subtle but profound. We are not only to make disciples in all the world but also to disciple nations. Wait, you might ask, are you saying that we are to take over all the spheres of influence in our nation and institute a theocracy over our government? No, what I am saying is that we can have a great effect on all the spheres of influence and elect people to public office who will legislate based on godly values and not from valueless, humanistic, and ungodly ideologies. Someone is always going to make the rules, whether they be righteous or not.

BE OF GOOD COURAGE

Let me ask you a pointed question. Why do we as people who love God and diligently try to live lives that are pleasing to Him tend to, in the name of acceptance and tolerance, have to tolerate every godless philosophy and deviant practice that radical ideologues feel entitled to foist upon our nation? We are not beholden to accept unrighteousness in the name of "toleration." Quite the opposite; God has given His children a mandate to "disciple nations." If the

AMERICA: LOST AND FOUND

Christians in ancient Rome were able to influence such an idolatrous iron-fisted regime, to the point that the Empire eventually declared Christianity as the official religion, should not we have the same influence in America?

And remember, Rome was completely hostile to Christianity at its inception, murdering thousands in the Colosseum if they refused to worship Caesar as a god. On the other hand, we in America have been uniquely blessed at our founding to have the freedom to believe as our consciences direct us without fear of government oppression. We also were given the unheard-of privilege of electing our own leaders who were ultimately accountable to the people. I did not realize until recently that America, at its founding, was the only nation on earth where the people had the right to decide who its leaders would be. We, as Christians, must therefore be the gatekeepers of liberty and of promoting a populace that is far more a "moral and religious people" rather than a people with no restraint, who seek to codify every manner of godless lifestyle under the guise of democracy. We must educate and disciple the citizenry, especially our children, in the beliefs and values upon which this nation was founded.

That begs the question; do we as Christians really have a good grasp of the Constitutional rights we are privileged to have as American citizens? We hear often those on the far left accusing any who disagree with them as being those who are trying to destroy democracy. How many of us are factually aware that we don't live in a democracy? Democracy can reduce a nation to

CHAPTER 9: NOT OF THIS WORLD—PART 1

mob rule. In a democracy if 50% of the people plus one vote for anyone or anything, then it becomes established. Carried to its logical conclusion, in a democracy, there are no inalienable rights! That is far removed from the Constitutional Republic that America was established as. The mob has no right to take away anyone's constitutionally guaranteed rights.

However, all too often, too many of us have conceded our rights, believing that whatever the governing authorities dictate, we must obey so as not to be found as rebels. After all, doesn't the Bible tell us to obey "Rulers and authorities" (Titus 3:1)? In America, however, any governing authority that takes it upon itself to violate the rights of the citizens has overstepped its authority and has, indeed, violated the highest law of the land, thus making itself lawless and illegitimate. It is neither here nor there if those in government act lawlessly, willfully, or out of ignorance. If we as citizens are not aware of our rights and allow this overreach, we have done nothing but embolden those in authority to continue this lawless behavior to achieve whatever agenda they are pursuing.

So what is my point, you may be asking? We are not being rebellious to insist that those whom we elect and those who are employed in government positions, who receive their wages from the labor of our hands, not only to respect but zealously uphold the rights of the citizens. That is what is legal and right in America. Failure or refusal to respect and uphold those rights is what is illegal. So we must not be intimidated when standing for our legal rights. The words of British statesman Edmund Burke, "All evil needs to succeed is for good people to do nothing," are as timely today as they were during the colonial era.

It is worth reiterating the purpose of this book: to exhort, encourage, and edify the church to stand with humble confidence for the free proclamation of the good news, the Gospel of the Kingdom. In so doing we unashamedly embrace our identity as salt (preservative) and light (illumination of the Truth) and function in our position as Ambassadors of Christ.

EKKLESIA?

Let me take a minute to discuss the term Ekklesia. Undoubtedly many Christians understand the term, but I don't want to assume that everyone does. I, for one, only learned about it myself a few years ago, though I have been a Christian for more than forty years. It is a powerful term that Jesus employed to describe His Body. In virtually all English translations, the body of believers is referred to as "the Church," indicative of a congregation, which is partly true. However, of the over 115 references to the Body of Christ, only three use the word translated "Church." All the rest use the word Ekklesia.

Ekklesia is a Greek word which was also employed by the Romans. It refers to the governing body of elders in a city or region. This body was responsible for creating laws for their given geographical sphere, similar to our city councils and state assemblies. So when Jesus said, ". . . on

CHAPTER 9: NOT OF THIS WORLD—PART 1

this rock I will build My church (Ekklesia), and the gates of Hades shall not prevail against it" (Matthew 16:18, parenthesis added), He was establishing the identity of His disciples as a governing body, representing His government here on earth of which He is King. Remember when Pilate asked Jesus if He was King? Jesus answered, "It is as you say" (Luke 23:3).

We are His Ekklesia! We are His governing authority on earth! This has brought so much clarity as to why Jesus so often declared the Kingdom of God was at hand. Because it was. He was in the process of establishing His Embassy, if you will, not in the form of a geographical location, because His Kingdom is not tied to a specific place, but rather a representative body of His disciples. This representative body would function as Ambassadors on earth in the form of an Ekklesia, a governing body empowered to enforce the will of the King over all opposing rulers of darkness. What would be the intended outcome? Nothing less than the discipling of nations.

That mandate was given to us when He said, "I give you authority to trample on serpents and scorpions and over all the power of the enemy" (Luke 10:19 emphasis added). This is our authorization as His governing body on earth to confront principalities and powers on earth through prayer, intercession, and declarations. Quite a different identity and function than that which refers to us merely as a congregation of Christians gathering for Sunday service! More on this later.

For me, this identity as a member of His Ekklesia,

completely changed how I viewed myself and the Body of Christ. Our role had changed from that of congregation to active members of Christ's governing assembly here on earth.

Let me clarify. I am not saying that our position is to physically take over and rule earthly governments—although by our mere presence and influence that could be the effective outcome. *Influence* is the operative word here. We saw how the influence of the believers in the Roman Empire affected the eventual transition from a pagan culture to that of a predominantly Christian one. Obviously, there are many caveats as to how Christian Rome turned out; nevertheless, the culture was dramatically changed for the better. And that is the point. The more that we function in our spiritual authority as the government of God on earth, the more we will see the influence of the Kingdom of God manifest in the various spheres of influence in our world: government, economy, culture, education, spiritual matters, media, and so on.

Let us take hold of this great privilege of being His representative government, His ambassadors here on earth. We exercise our authority as the Ekklesia, empowered by the Holy Spirit, to participate in the salvation of the peoples and transformation of the nations.

SHORTEN YOUR MEMORY

Brethren, I do not count myself to have apprehended; but one thing I do, forgetting those things which are behind

CHAPTER 9: NOT OF THIS WORLD—PART 1

and reaching forward to those things which are ahead, I press toward the goal for the prize of the upward call of God in Christ Jesus (Philippians 3:13-14).

The upward call wasn't meant for the Apostle Paul alone. Each of us has an upward call of God in Christ Jesus.

> For I say, through the grace given to me, to everyone who is among you, not to think of himself more highly than he ought to think, but to think soberly, as God has dealt to each one a measure of faith (Romans 12:3).
> For I know the thoughts that I think toward you, says the Lord, thoughts of peace and not of evil, to give you a future and a hope (Jeremiah 29:11).

The issue isn't whether or not we each have a call from God on our lives; that issue is forever settled. He has called each of us and has established plans for every individual member of His family. Rather the issue is have we esteemed it as God's call or have we considered it less significant because we are not a Paul, or a Peter, or a John? Did not Paul say that he dared not go beyond his sphere of influence and that he did not want to build on another man's work? Since Paul recognized that he had specific assignments from God, shouldn't we as well?

> For we are His workmanship, created in Christ Jesus for *good works*, which God prepared beforehand that we should walk in them (Ephesians 2:10).

This is the affirming, accepting, and security-infusing promise that God wants us to embrace, because, it is the truth, and Jesus said the truth would set us free. God did not say that He prepared good *beliefs* for us to walk in, important as believing the truths contained in the Word of God are; He said that He prepared good *works* for us to walk in. In other words, He expects us to take action!

. . . but the people who know their God shall be strong, and carry out great exploits (Daniel 11:32).

So each of us needs to find out what God means by "exploits and good works" He has called us to do. As I look back, I can recall many missed opportunities to have ministered "good works." Two very different lessons can be learned from these "missed opportunities." I can either feel discouraged, regretful, and disqualified for future service to the Lord, or as Paul advises, I can ask for and receive forgiveness from the Lord and move on, ". . . forgetting those things which are behind and reaching forward to those things which are ahead" (Philippians 3:13). If we have confessed our sins and failures to the Lord, going forward He will have no remembrance of them, so what point is there in us continuing to ruminate on them? Shorten your memory!

WORKS? WHAT ABOUT GRACE?

Although stated earlier, I believe this bears repeating: our "good works" have no bearing on our status as saved sons and daughters of God. Salvation is received not earned. Christ earned our salvation for us because we could not

CHAPTER 9: NOT OF THIS WORLD—PART 1

earn it for ourselves. We received our salvation when we believed and confessed Christ:

> ... if you confess with your mouth the Lord Jesus and believe in your heart that God has raised Him from the dead, you will be saved (Romans 10:9).

Good works are the result of salvation and not the means to attain it.

> But someone will say, "You have faith, and I have works." Show me your faith without your works, and I will show you my faith by my works" (James 2:18).

This verse is often misinterpreted to claim that James is saying that works are necessary for your salvation. That is not at all his intent, and it is certainly not true. James firmly believes that "good works" are the result of salvation. However, he refuses to let believers "off the hook" thinking that they have no need of demonstrable fruit in their lives. What James is saying is that if you have been born again, you will as a result bear good fruit. If there is no recognizable fruit, it calls into question whether you actually have experienced the transformation that the new birth in Christ precipitates.

> The fruit of the Spirit is love, joy, peace, longsuffering, kindness, goodness, faithfulness, gentleness, self-control (Galatians 5:22).

If this fruit is present in our lives, will it not show itself? Should not the "good works, which God prepared beforehand that we should walk in them" be evident every day of our lives? We often fail to realize just how evident the fruit of the Spirit is in our lives, especially if we have walked with the Lord for many years.

When I consider the manner in which I now treat people since I was born again, I see an elevated amount of care, preference, consideration, and value for others than compared to that which I walked in prior to my salvation. We can be encouraged that, though this may not seem such a significant manifestation of the fruit of the Spirit, it really is.

> If a brother or sister is naked and destitute of daily food, and one of you says to them, "Depart in peace, be warmed and filled," but you do not give them the things which are needed for the body, what does it profit? Thus also faith by itself, if it does not have works, is dead. (James 2:15-17)

The good works "that we should walk in" can easily manifest in practical ways when we see our brothers and sisters in need, whether physical or spiritual, and take the steps necessary to meet those needs.

Years ago I was at a Vineyard conference, when John Wimber related an account of a man, a member of the church, who approached him at the end of a Sunday service. He told John how he came to the church building

CHAPTER 9: NOT OF THIS WORLD—PART 1

midweek, but it seemed that no one was there. As he was leaving, he noticed a man rummaging through the dumpster. He gave the man some money and, I believe, bought him some food as well. After telling this story he asked John a question, "Isn't the church supposed to take care of that kind of thing?" John responded with one of the wisest answers I had ever heard. He said to the man, "It sounds to me like the church did."

This beautifully illustrates what it looks like to walk into the "good works God prepared beforehand that we should walk in them." How often do we not see the one right in front of us?

About five years ago I was coming out of the drugstore and a man was sitting outside who appeared to be African-American. I noticed that he had a shopping cart full of his belongings. I briefly exchanged small talk and pleasantries, said goodbye and God bless you, and if I recall correctly, he blessed me in return. As I drove away, I thought, "I should have given him some money." In less than two minutes I returned to the drugstore, and he had left. Given his age and the fact he was pushing his shopping cart, I knew he should have still been fairly close by. So I started driving down the streets closest to the drugstore expanding my route to over a quarter of a mile; but I couldn't find him anywhere. I didn't see how in less than three minutes he could have traveled so far. Later, after returning home, I was kind of scolding myself that I hadn't given him the money at the time of our conversation. Still perplexed by the fact that I wasn't able to find him, the

AMERICA: LOST AND FOUND

thought came to me: did I just have an encounter with an angel? It could happen.

> Do not forget to entertain strangers, for by so doing some have unwittingly entertained angels. (Hebrews 13:2)

CHAPTER 10
NOT OF THIS WORLD— PART 2

Therefore, since all these things will be dissolved, what manner of persons ought you to be in holy conduct and godliness . . . (2 Peter 3:11)?

Finally, my brethren, be strong in the Lord and in the power of His might. Put on the whole armor of God, that you may be able to stand against the wiles of the devil. For we do not wrestle against flesh and blood, but against principalities, against powers, against the rulers of the darkness of this age, against spiritual hosts of wickedness in the heavenly places. Therefore, take up the whole armor of God, that you may be able to withstand in the evil day, and having done all, to stand (Ephesians 6:10-13).

Since most of us have not seen with our own eyes the host of Heaven or the demonic principalities and rulers of wickedness in high places, it becomes easy to go about our daily lives with little or no awareness that these angelic beings are prevalent. But, whether for good or evil, they are real and are interacting with us either for our good or our hurt. This is, nevertheless, the reality we must grasp and operate in if we are to be successful in waging a good warfare.

We don't have to see the chariots of God as Elisha's servant did when the Lord revealed the host of heaven to him in 2 Kings 6:17, to recognize the opposite to be true, that spiritual hosts of wickedness are fully arrayed in an all-out firefight with us. Their agenda is to turn our nation from its roots of devotion to God to worshiping and obeying the god of this world, Satan. Certainly, issues and persons on the governmental front must be addressed and dealt with in the natural. But these are merely manifesting the result of being manipulated by the "Prince of the power of the air" (Ephesians 2:2), through his deceptions and incitements to do evil.

> For though we walk in the flesh, we do not war according to the flesh. For the weapons of our warfare are not carnal but mighty in God for pulling down strongholds, casting down arguments and every high thing that exalts itself against the knowledge of God, bringing every thought into captivity to the obedience of Christ (2 Corinthians 10:3-5).

PRAY THE WORD

Just as Nehemiah rebuilt the wall of Jerusalem with a sword in one hand, so do we, as we bring the Kingdom

CHAPTER 10: NOT OF THIS WORLD—PART 2

of God into the spheres of influence in our daily lives. Wield the "Sword of the Spirit, which is the Word of God" (Ephesians 6:17). Through intercession and decreeing the truths and promises of God over our families, friends, workplaces, and every area in which we are involved, we can release Kingdom influence.

> Isaiah 55:11 says, "So shall My word be that goes forth from My mouth; It shall not return to Me void, But it shall accomplish what I please, And it shall prosper in the thing for which I sent it."
>
> Job 22:26-28 says, "For then you will have your delight in the Almighty, And lift up your face to God. You will make your prayer to Him, He will hear you, And you will pay your vows. You will also declare a thing, And it will be established for you; So light will shine on your ways."

These verses reveal powerful truths and promises that combine to form potent spiritual weapons in our arsenal. I was first exposed to the power of praying the actual Word of God and the power of decrees over fifteen years ago. Since God's Word does not return void but will accomplish what He has sent it out to do, praying His Word as part of our intercession can deliver powerful results. Remember the value God places on His own Word, "For You have magnified Your word above all Your name" (Psalm 138:2).

2 Peter 1:2-4 speaks of the precious promises of God to enable us to be partakers of His divine nature:

Grace and peace be multiplied to you in the knowledge of God and of Jesus our Lord, as His divine power has given to us all things that pertain to life and godliness, through the knowledge of Him who called us by glory and virtue, by which have been given to us exceedingly great and precious promises, that through these you may be partakers of the divine nature, having escaped the corruption that is in the world through lust.

For all the promises of God in Him are Yes, and in Him Amen, to the glory of God through us (2 Corinthians 1:20).

Here are some promises that we can appropriate in our intercessory prayers: "Your Kingdom come. Your will be done on earth as it is in Heaven" (Matthew 6:10).

This, I believe, is the most universal part of the Lord's Prayer. I pray this nearly every day. I apply it to America, my household, my marriage, my children and grandchildren, and anything thing else I desire His Kingdom to come upon and His will to be done in.

So they said, "Believe on the Lord Jesus Christ, and you will be saved, you and your household" (Acts 16:31).

Pray and declare this scripture over your household. I pray this often over my immediate and extended family, as well as friends of my household. Since God can do "exceedingly, abundantly above all we ask or think" (Ephesians 3:20), and since "God is not willing that any should perish"

CHAPTER 10: NOT OF THIS WORLD—PART 2

(2 Peter 3:9), I don't limit my prayer to just those of my immediate family, but I extend the blessing of salvation to everyone who is in any way related to my "household."

Consider the intercession of John the Apostle:

> Beloved, I pray that you may prosper in all things and be in health, just as your soul prospers (3 John 1:2).

"But isn't this akin the name it and claim it, health and wealth gospel?" I assume here, that John the Apostle was not praying for anything that was outside of God's will. After all, this is scripture.

So if our souls are prospering (growing) in the Lord, then we can have confidence to pray in agreement with the Word that we will also prosper and be in good health as a result. I pray something along the lines of "Lord, as my soul prospers in You, I thank You that You will cause me to prosper and be in good health." The manner and type of blessings are entirely up to the Lord, but let's not miss out on receiving "every good and perfect gift" (James 1:17) that our Father wants to give us.

I have found that the more I look at the Word of God in the light of being a volume that displays His great and precious promises, the more confidence I have that "all God's promises in Him (Christ) are yes and amen" (2 Corinthians 1:20, parentheses added).

Numerous scriptures are direct promises that we can pray to see manifested in our lives. When you read the Word, I encourage you to see with new eyes. And, in case you feel that you are being presumptuous in declaring the Word of God over your life, remember Jesus said, "Ask and you will receive" (John 16:24). Again, remember that it is the Lord who declares:

> So shall My word be that goes forth from My mouth; It shall not return to Me void, But it shall accomplish what I please, And it shall prosper in the thing for which I sent it (Isaiah 55:11).

BINDING AND LOOSING

Much has been said about binding and loosing, but for our purposes, we will just take the plain meaning as it was spoken by Jesus. He is granting a new level of authority to His disciples that, here to fore, had not been available to mankind since the fall.

> And I will give you the keys of the kingdom of heaven, and whatever you bind on earth will be bound in heaven, and whatever you loose on earth will be loosed in heaven (Matthew 16:19).

It may appear in this verse, that Jesus is delegating this authority to Peter alone and not to the disciples as a whole. However, Jesus uses this same verbiage in Matthew 18:18, when He is addressing all the disciples. We can glean from this that the Lord is establishing a new standard that will apply to all who will ever follow Him.

CHAPTER 10: NOT OF THIS WORLD—PART 2

One of the greatest examples of spiritual warfare, which is often cited, is from Daniel 10:12-13:

> Then he said to me, "Do not fear, Daniel, for from the first day that you set your heart to understand, and to humble yourself before your God, your words were heard; and I have come because of your words. But the prince of the kingdom of Persia withstood me twenty-one days; and behold, Michael, one of the chief princes, came to help me, for I had been left alone there with the kings of Persia."

Daniel did not possess the authority to bind and loose on his own, but through his intercession, God answered and sent an angelic messenger, who needed assistance from the Archangel Michael to bring Daniel the answer to his prayers. I don't know of any passage in scripture that more clearly reveals the war that is fought in the heavens and how it affects us here on earth more than this account does.

Intercession is still the primary means by which we can conduct spiritual warfare. Jesus, however, adds to our intercession a more powerful aspect. We are given direct authority to bind the operation of "spiritual wickedness." No longer are we solely dependent on angels to fight for us, as in the account in Daniel, but we are now authorized to engage with the enemy ourselves.

> I have given you authority to trample on snakes and scorpions and to overcome all the power of the enemy; nothing will harm you (Luke 10:19).

> For we do not wrestle against flesh and blood, but against principalities, against powers, against the rulers of the darkness of this age, against spiritual hosts of wickedness in the heavenly places (Ephesians 6:12).
>
> Are not all angels ministering spirits sent to serve those who will inherit salvation (Hebrews 1:14)?

Having been given this authority to overcome all the power of the enemy, we can exercise our right to bind demonic influence and operation as the Lord's Ekklesia. And as we are instructed to pray, "Your Kingdom come and Your will be done on earth as it is in heaven," we can safely pray for the "loosing" of angels to be dispatched to serve and minister to and for us in the warfare in which we are engaged. When I first grasped this revelation, it was a major "ah-ha" moment. What an amazing position and privilege God has bestowed on us! I am also quick to remember that "For everyone to whom much is given much is required" (Luke 12:48). Let us steward well this privilege and responsibility.

PRACTICAL APPLICATION

This binding and loosing mandate, as we see in Matthew 18:18, can be applied to practical situations and not exclusively to spiritual warfare.

Having first interceded, exercising our authority as the Lord's governing body on earth, the Ekklesia, what then can we be about in bringing the influence of the Kingdom

CHAPTER 10: NOT OF THIS WORLD—PART 2

of God into the earth and into the process of disciplining nations?

As mentioned earlier in this book, we as Americans have been given the incredible privilege to select our governmental leaders through the election process. As Christians, I have no doubt that we bear a serious responsibility before the Lord to avail ourselves of this privilege. Knowing that God ordained the creation of this nation to be a beacon of the Gospel to the world, how could we think otherwise?[1]

The fact is that many evangelical, as well as many mainline Christian's votes, are split between conservative and leftist candidates, particularly in the presidential races. In 2020, combining white and non-white evangelicals, about 70% voted Republican. Amongst mainline denominations, the vote was split almost evenly with Republicans receiving 52% of the vote. White and non-white Catholics voted approximately 52% Republican. This would put the percentage of professing Christians, whether Protestant or Catholic, who voted Democrat or another party at approximately 40%.[2] What is more significant is that the number of registered voters who identify as Christian has dropped 15% from 2008 to 2020.[3]

Combining these percentages, we see millions of votes either cast for candidates who espouse and, more importantly, legislate utterly anti-biblical beliefs, as discussed in previous chapters, or are simply lost due to the failure to just vote.

A revival resulting in a majority of Christians embracing

the command of Jesus to "Seek first the Kingdom of God and His righteousness" (Matthew 6:33) and abandon the weak and insipid cultural Christianity, which has "A form of godliness, but denies the power thereof" (2 Timothy 3:5) would result in an insurmountable block of voters who would settle for nothing less than godly character from its elected leaders. "Righteousness exalts a nation, but sin is a reproach to any people" (Proverbs 14:34).

I would challenge any true disciple of Christ to consider how he/she would answer the Lord if He were to hypothetically ask "Why did you vote for candidates who endorse and facilitate the murder of millions of human beings created in My image, through abortion?" Do you think that an acceptable response would be, "Well, I was willing to overlook issues like abortion, sexually deviant indoctrination of school children, and cultural indoctrination related to transgenderism because my concern for certain social issues promoted by certain candidates took precedence?"

To make your mark on the ballot sheet for those who advocate, legislate, and fund abortion is to put yourself in agreement with those who are willing proponents of killing, stealing, and destroying life. I ask you, who else might that put you in agreement with? Don't shoot the messenger. We will all give an account of what we have agreed with. My motivation here is that no brother or sister in Christ—or anyone else for that matter—need be ashamed before the Lord of how they would have to answer that question.

CHAPTER 10: NOT OF THIS WORLD—PART 2

We must vote to put into office those who most espouse and adhere to godly, biblical values, and we must use our vote as a weapon. At the very least, if you cannot bring yourself to vote for a certain candidate, never default to voting for a blatantly ungodly one!

POLITICAL CORRECTNESS OR DISCERNING CORRECTLY?

No matter how culturally unpopular biblical beliefs and values have been painted by those with the microphones, and those in academia, we as followers of Christ must stand with an unwavering commitment to believing and proclaiming the truth, which is the Word of God. We just can't continue to succumb to the censorship of political correctness. I never quite understood what political correctness was and how it was determined that it was correct in the first place. But wait, we have a definition from Britannica:

The term first appeared in Marxist-Leninist vocabulary following the Russian Revolution of 1917. At that time it was used to describe adherence to the policies and principles of the Communist Party of the Soviet Union (that is, the party line).[4] So when it comes to giving credence to the idea of "political correctness" we should employ the maxim: "Consider the source." In this case, the source is Marxist communism.

Years ago, I realized that the concept of political correctness was being used as a weapon to silence any who disagreed with godless leftist ideologies and paradigms. It conveniently labeled its opponents as racists, homophobes, transphobes, and you-name-it "phobes"! Effectively shutting down any opposing views before an intelligent discussion of the merits of both sides of a given issue could even begin. I also realized that my views warranted as much consideration as any with opposing viewpoints. Therefore, those initiating actions to suppress my right to free speech amounted to nothing short of oppression in the form of censorship. And the ones most responsible for such censorship are the media, social and broadcast.

All this is to say that the desired effect of those using "political correctness" (PC) as a weapon has in large part been achieved. I can't tell how many times I have, along with many other believers, said something of a logical and commonsensical nature only to back-peddle and say, "I guess that's not politically correct." The tactic of silencing the opposition by the PC crowd to promote any number of specious ideologies, that for the greater part of history either never existed or were fringe ideas at best, has been most effective. However, as possessors of the truth, we need to begin with "speaking the truth in love" (Ephesians 4:15). Some will be willing to engage in honest discourse, but many will not. The former may be won by hearing the truth as "faith comes by hearing and hearing by the Word of God." The latter, although initially opposing the truth, may nevertheless not be able to resist the truth seeds that have been planted. The type of soil will determine the eventual outcome. Either way, plant we must.

CHAPTER 10: NOT OF THIS WORLD—PART 2

ENDURING TO THE END

I must admit that what has been an overwhelming wave of ungodliness in our country has at times caused me to want to just hunker down until, by whatever circumstances, I go be with the Lord. But I, and we, have not been afforded that option. Jesus said that we are to be "salt and light," and we were to be like "a city set on a hill whose light cannot be hidden" and "a lamp set on a lampstand giving light to all who are in the house" (Matthew 5:13-16).

I love one of the lines uttered by the character Gandalf in the first *Lord of the Rings* film. In answering Frodo's lament that he "wished none of this had ever happened," Gandalf replies with empathy and great wisdom, "None of us wish for times such as these, Frodo, but ours is not to choose the times that have come upon us; it is only ours to decide what to do with the time that is given."

As I look back at just over forty-five years of being saved, I consider how much time was not well spent in being fruitful for the Kingdom. I'm sure there is much fruit that I have indeed produced but have forgotten about or did not personally get to see the harvest. This tendency to look back and lament over the past has never been a good vehicle for encouraging me to have much hope and vision for the time I have left. However, if each of us had only one day left, would it be worth investing that time into expanding the Kingdom? Two results would be assured. First, the Lord would be pleased, "for without faith, it is impossible to please God" (Hebrews 11:6), and second, we would receive a greater reward.

Part of the motivation for writing this book was that I wanted not only to be obedient to what I believed the Lord wanted me to do but to continue to be fruitful until my assignment here is finished. Please don't think that because you may only have a few years left it's too late to do anything significant for the Lord. If you led one family member or friend to the Lord, which causes the angels in Heaven to rejoice, you have helped birth another son or daughter for the Lord and increased the reward for which He sacrificed Himself. Honestly, I believe that all of us who love Him can easily do a lot more than that with the time we have left. Since God prepared good works that we should walk in, there is no reason to think that we have exhausted the personal list He has for each of us until He calls us home. When He said, "Be fruitful and multiply," He did not put a cap on the command at sixty, seventy, eighty, or even ninety years of age.

It's not a burden to serve the Lord; it is an honor. One that includes great rewards. The best earthly employers cannot begin to compete with the "perks" that the Lord promises.

Finally, there is laid up for me the crown of righteousness, which the Lord, the righteous Judge, will give to me on that Day, and not to me only, also to all who have loved His appearing (2 Timothy 4:8).

... as His divine power has given to us all things that pertain to life and godliness, through the knowledge of Him

CHAPTER 10: NOT OF THIS WORLD—PART 2

who called us by glory and virtue, by which have been given to us exceedingly great and precious promises, that through these you may be partakers of the divine nature. (2 Peter: 3-4)

ON TO VICTORY

So just as it was true for Elisha, it remains true for us today. "Do not fear, for those who are with us are more than those who are with them" (2 Kings 6:16). The writer of Hebrews exhorts us to consider the role of angels:

"Are they not all ministering spirits (angels) sent forth to minister for those who will inherit salvation" (Hebrews 1:14). We are also surrounded by the "Great Cloud of Witnesses" (Hebrews 12:1). Those who've gone ahead who are cheering us on.

How much greater is that truth now that we have been given the keys to the Kingdom of God, are joint heirs with Christ, and are called to be His Ambassadors! I continually must remind myself what my identity is and who I truly am in Christ, and so should we all. Great is the honor, glory, and position the Lord has given us. As John the Apostle says in 1 John 3:1, "Behold what manner of love the Father has bestowed on us, that we should be called children of God!"

It is a hard thing to settle in our thinking, but those who are in and of the world are under the influence and thereby the control of the enemy, and because of that, many of them reject and/or hate us.

If the world hates you, you know that it hated Me before it hated you. If you were of the world, the world would love its own. Yet because you are not of the world, but I chose you out of the world, therefore the world hates you (John 15:17-19).

In a war, the combatants often possess a vehement hatred of each other. Certainly, our enemy the devil hates us, as do those under his sway. However, one of the great Kingdom paradoxes is that we are called to "love our enemies." We do that by blessing them, praying for them, and speaking the truth to them in love. Our victory comes not by killing, as in conventional warfare, but by bringing people to faith in Jesus. With each new birth in Christ, they are saved from death and Satan suffers a great defeat. If God is not willing that any should perish, then neither should we.

This brings me to the conclusion of what I wanted to communicate through this book. "We are more than conquerors through Him who loved us" (Romans 8:37), and we have a mandate from our Lord to preach the Kingdom of God and to make disciples of all nations. He has recreated us through the new birth in Christ and given us His Holy Spirit and power to accomplish this.

I often call to mind that in World War II, D-Day was the actual day that the outcome of the war was determined. The Allies would win the war. We, like them, are merely fighting a mop-up operation, liberating those who have been taken captive by the enemy. The enemy hasn't given

CHAPTER 10: NOT OF THIS WORLD—PART 2

up fighting, and there will be casualties still, but the outcome of the war we are engaged in was determined at the cross of and by the resurrection of Jesus. So "Do not fear, little flock, for it is your Father's good pleasure to give you the kingdom" (Luke 12:32).

Much of the content of this book was spent describing what America has lost. What is to be found can be revealed by God's children kindling new fires of love, devotion, and passion for Jesus. As we assume the vantage position of a "city set on a hill," we can see the entire surrounding territory that lies in darkness; we can also see that America can begin to be drawn back by that light. We are a chosen people, blessed beyond any nation in history. That we have been blessed materially is obvious. But even that is due to the foundation of being a nation that was dedicated to the Glory of God and the proclamation of the Gospel throughout the earth. Historically, many nations of the world have possessed equivalent natural resources as us but have been mired in tyranny, corruption, injustice, and poverty. For the majority of our history, we have been a nation whose overarching belief system and cultural norms were rooted in the Christian faith. Our form of government, our laws, and our system of justice were all formed based on the commands and directives of scripture. Determining to stand, and refusing to bow the knee to the rampant depravity and godlessness that so deeply infects us at present, we can once again witness the return of our wonderful country to being "One nation under God." Our best years, indeed, are right ahead of us.

AMERICA: LOST AND FOUND

So let us, as we are instructed in Hebrews 12:1 "... lay aside every weight, and the sin which so easily ensnares us, and let us run with endurance the race that is set before us."

And until the final victory is realized, "Be strong and of good courage; do not be afraid, nor be dismayed, for the LORD your God *is* with you wherever you go" (Joshua 1:9).[5]

CHAPTER 11
AND ANOTHER THING

There are many ways that we can act to affect the course and direction of America going forward. As previously discussed, it always starts with intercession. Praying for and anticipating another Great Awakening, beginning with the church, is where we start. An old radio program that I faithfully listened to as a new believer opened every broadcast with the phrase "God is still on the throne, and prayer changes things." This is how we start our engines, by "appealing to Heaven" just as George Washington did during the Revolutionary War.

> Let us therefore come boldly to the throne of grace, that we may obtain mercy and find grace to help in time of need (Hebrews 4:16).

Having begun our assault on the enemy by entering the throne room of Heaven, let's discuss some more practical measures. We have already talked about the great privilege we have been given as American citizens, that of voting for those whom we want to lead us. Now let's take it up a notch or two. Already many devoted followers of Christ are attending city-council and school-board meetings to voice their concerns about various measures that these governing bodies are proposing or implementing in our cities and public schools.

Consider attending a few of these meetings, first to get educated on meeting procedures and secondly, how to have your voice heard within the rules and procedures of these gatherings. This is also a right afforded to us as citizens. Although you may meet resistance from some of the elected officials, one thing is sure, when they start seeing that a sizable number of their constituents are voicing similar concerns, they will begin to listen more closely, some for no other reason than wanting to keep their jobs!

On the school front, many parents recognizing the abhorrent agendas being injected into their children's schools have become volunteers in the classroom to keep a close watch on what is being taught and promoted. I encourage any parent whose schedule permits to do the same. Teachers are generally very appreciative of the help. Your presence means that, in your interactions with the children, you can influence them toward godly values, and quietly pray for them as well.

Other Christians are diving into the deep end and running for city-council and school-board seats. Others who have been involved in public office for a longer period of time have run for and won many county, state, and federal offices. While it's good and effective to engage in discourse

CHAPTER 11: AND ANOTHER THING

with leaders pursuing ungodly legislation in governmental meetings, it is even more effective to remove and replace them altogether. Now at this point, I'm pretty sure that the last sentence caused a twinge in some of you because the thought of getting involved on this level has occurred to you and will incur cost. Nevertheless considering what is at stake, I urge you to pray into it. That twinge just might be from the Holy Spirit and not just something you ate for dinner last night.

Many Christians are familiar with the teaching commonly known as the "Seven Mountains of Influence" in society. Well-known Christian leaders such as Loren Cunningham, Bill Bright, Lance Wallnau, and Johnny Enlow have taught and promoted this concept. It essentially identifies the seven spheres of cultural influence as Religion, Family, Education, Government, Media, Arts and Entertainment, and Business.

I'm sure that every one of us is involved in one or more of these areas of influence. So what does that mean, you ask? Well, consider the apostle Paul, who I affectionately refer to as the "All Time Number One Christian Dude." He provided for himself in the "Mountain of Business" as a tent maker in the marketplace. He used his occupation as an opportunity to preach the Gospel to those he was associated with and had built relationships with. This is how many New Testament Ekklesias (churches) were established. Similarly, Dorcas (a seamstress), Lydia (a trader in dye) and Cornelius (a Roman centurion) were all marketplace leaders who, on coming to Christ, became significant influencers of the gospel in their communities (Acts 9:36-43; 10:1).

I have tried to employ this mindset wherever I worked in the marketplace, but often later realized I had checked in my Ambassadorship at the door. Most of our occupational positions require tremendous focus, and it is not surprising that we can find ourselves so immersed in just being faithful to fulfilling the demands of the job that we can lose sight of operating out of our true identity, that of being first and foremost, disciples of Christ, and how I can function as one without neglecting the other.

This integration of roles, regardless of what our spheres of influence are, is what Paul modeled for us perfectly. It has become woefully apparent that a substantial portion of the Body of Christ has, at best, not successfully achieved this integration, or at worst, neglected it altogether. Think about what the Word says about who the actual ministers are in the Body of Christ, the Ekklesia.

> And He Himself gave some to be apostles, some prophets, some evangelists, and some pastors and teachers, for the equipping of the saints for the work of ministry, for the edifying of the Body of Christ (Ephesians 4:11-12).

As much as we Christians profess to understand this verse, we still tend to think of the true ministers in the church as those who are full-time professional staff. Unfortunately, many in church leadership, often unknowingly, promote this idea. But carefully consider the purpose of the offices

CHAPTER 11: AND ANOTHER THING

described in this verse. The sole purpose of the "five-fold ministry" is to equip the saints, all born-again believers, for the work of the ministry. What is the ministry? Although serving within the confines of "church" gatherings and meetings is ministry, it is a secondary ministry, only needed to support the primary ministry which is preaching the Gospel of the Kingdom. All these preeminent ministry offices are given to serve this one overarching purpose.

Consider how exponentially more powerful it would be if the entire Body of Christ engaged in expanding the Kingdom of God as opposed to heavily relying upon the "Professional Clergy" to do the work. This is where we, as disciples of Christ, need to fix our gaze and begin to consistently pray into. As more and more of us receive this revelation of our role as followers of Jesus and apply it to whatever our spheres of influence are, we may quickly see an unexpected and an amazing level of societal transformation.

> Do you not know that those who run in a race all run, but one receives the prize? Run in such a way that you may obtain it (1 Corinthians 9:24).
> Therefore, we also, since we are surrounded by so great a cloud of witnesses, let us lay aside every weight, and the sin which so easily ensnares us, and let us run with endurance the race that is set before us (Hebrews 12:1).

My sincere desire is for this book to be an encouraging rallying call to action for the Body of Christ. Let it rekindle

AMERICA: LOST AND FOUND

the fires in each of us that may have lost some of their intensity. As we embrace our high calling of God in Christ Jesus, I believe we will begin to see and experience firsthand what it is to become the "glorious church" of Ephesians 5:27 that Jesus is longing for and will be returning for.

RESOURCES

The following links are provided to give the reader practical ways to increase effectiveness as the Ekklesia and have a greater influence on the world around for the Kingdom of God.

Intercession:
https://www.givehim15.com/
https://www.youtube.com/results?search_query=give+him+15+dutch+sheets
https://ifapray.org/

Fighting child sex trafficking:
ourrescue.org
timtebowfoundation.org
love146.org

Evangelistic and transformative ministries:
transformourworld.org
globalcelebration.com
irisglobal.org

AMERICA: LOST AND FOUND

Legal organizations advocating for righteousness:
aclj.org
judicialwatch.org

END NOTES

All Scripture references, unless otherwise noted, are from the: New King James Version (NKJV), Thomas Nelson Publishers, 1975.

INTRODUCTION

1. Christianity in the United States, https://en.wikipedia.org/wiki/Christianity_in_the_United_States, Last revision December 30, 2023.

2. Percentage of Christian registered voters drops 15% since 2008: Pew, By Jackson Elliott, Christian Post Reporter, https://www.christianpost.com/news/percentage-of-christian-voters-drops-15-since-2008-pew.html, November 5, 2020.

CHAPTER 1

1. John W. Whitehead, The Second American Revolution (Elgin, IL: David C. Cook, 1982) p. 75.

2. Ibid., p. 75.

3. https://www.uwlax.edu/currents/how-often-do-people-lie/

4. https://www.zippia.com/advice/employee-theft-statistics/

5. Dr. Martin Luther King Jr., https://www.beliefnet.com/quotes/inspiration/m/martin-luther-king-jr/if-a-man-is-called-to-be-a-streetsweeper-he-shoul.aspx

CHAPTER 2

1. Merriam-Webster https://www.merriam-webster.com/dictionary/acceptance

2. Dictioany.com, https://www.dictionary.com/browse/phobia

CHAPTER 3

1. The Scopes Trial: A battle between creationism and evolution in public schools, by Patricia E. Daniels, https://www.thoughtco.com/the-scopes-trial-1779247, August 21, 2019.

2. Over 1,000 Scientists Openly Dissent From Evolution Theory, by Alex Newman, https://thenewamerican.com/us/tech/over-1-000-scientists-openly-dissent-from-evolution-theory/, March 11, 2019.

3. "Human Beings: The Products of the Environment." Psychology Writing, 7 Aug. 2023, psychologywriting.com/human-beings-the-products-of-the-environment/. Accessed 26 Jan. 2024.

4. 30 Priceless Quotes From the Great Thomas Sowell, fee.org, February 28, 2023.

CHAPTER 4

1. https://www.usccb.org/issues-and-action/human-life-and-dignity/abortion/supreme-courts-response-to-the-question-when-does-life-begin

2. abort73.com, U.S. Abortion Statistics, para 2, March 2018

END NOTES

3. https://www.merriam-webster.com/dictionary/eugenics, December 21, 2023

4. Margaret Sanger's racist legacy lives on at Planned Parenthood, by Abby Johnson, https://www.washingtonexaminer.com/opinion/op-eds/margaret-sangers-racist-legacy-lives-on-at-planned-parenthood, May 15, 2021, 12:00 AM.

5. https://acpeds.org/position-statements/when-human-life-begins

6. Staff. (2017, May 17). Should Abortion be Legal? Retrieved March 22, 2018, from ProCon.org website: https://abortion.procon.org

7. https://papers.ssrn.com/sol3/papers.cfm?abstract_id=3973608

8. Staff. (2017, May 17). Should Abortion be Legal? Retrieved March 22, 2018, from ProCon.org website: https://abortion.procon.org

CHAPTER 5

1. The Common Sense Book of Baby and Child Care by Dr. Benjamin Spock. New York: Duell, Sloan, and Pearce, 1946.

2. https://www.savethechildren.org/us/charity-stories/child-trafficking-myths-vs-facts

3. The New Norm in K-12 Public Schools, by Keri D. Ingraham, https://www.discovery.org/education/2022/02/23/the-new-norm-in-k-12-public-schools/, Feb. 23, 2022.

4. https://www.desiringgod.org/articles/will-you-lose-your-faith-in-college

5. critical race theory, Written and fact-checked by the editors of Encyclopedia Britannica, https://www.britannica.com/topic/critical-race-theory, Last Updated: Dec 24, 2023.

6. Morgan Freeman Interview with Don Lemon, https://www.youtube.com/watch?v=StNCmODlag, June 3, 2014.

7. Vladimir Lenin Quotes. BrainyQuote.com, BrainyMedia Inc, 2024. https://www.brainyquote.com/quotes/vladimir_lenin_153238, accessed February 1, 2024.

8. Sexually transmitted diseases in the USA: temporal trends, Sevgi O Aral, Kevin A Fenton, and King K Holmes, https://www.ncbi.nlm.nih.gov/pmc/articles/PMC2598671/, July 2007.

9. Promoting Porn In School Libraries Is The Real Problem, Not 'Banned Books', by Stephanie Lundquist-Arora, The Federalist, https://thefederalist.com/2023/10/02/promoting-porn-in-school-libraries-is-the-real-problem-not-banned-books/, October 2, 2023.

CHAPTER 6

1. https://en.wikipedia.org/wiki/Gender_dysphoria

2. https://en.wikipedia.org/wiki/Sex_differences_in_human_physiology

3. https://ny1.com/nyc/all-boroughs/news/2022/06/10/study-estimates-transgender-youth-population-has-doubled-in-5-years

4. Gender-Diverse and Transgender Children, by Jason Rafferty MD, https://www.healthychildren.org/English/ages-stages/gradeschool/Pages/Gender-Diverse-Transgender-Children.aspx, last updated June 8, 2022.

5. School boards want some perturbed parents branded domestic terrorists, by Robby Soave, https://reason.com/2021/10/06/ag-merrick-garland-fbi-critical-race-theory-parents-schools-domestic-terrorists/, October 6, 2021.

END NOTES

6. Treatment, Gender dysphoria, https://www.nhs.uk/conditions/gender-dysphoria/treatment/, last reviewed May 28, 2020.

7. The Downsides of Financial Incentives to Diagnose COVID | Opinion, Newsweek.com, Jan. 26, 2023.

8. California Family Council, Parents Publicly Expose Secret Elementary LGBTQ Clubs in Elk Grove, Greg Burt, https://www.californiafamily.org/2024/03/parents-set-to-publicly-expose-secret-elementary-lgbtq-clubs-in-elk-grove/, March 6, 2024.

CHAPTER 7

1. America's Covenant with God, http://1607covenant.com/, 2018.

2. The Founding Fathers, by Gordon Leidner, Published by Cumberland House, as an imprint of Sourcebooks, Inc. 2013.

3. Jefferson's Wall of Separation, Jan. 1, 1802 letterhttps://usconstitution.net/jeffwall.html, December 20, 2023.

4. W. Herbert Burk, B. D., Washington's Prayers, (Norristown, Penn.: Published for the Benefit of the Washington Memorial Chapel, 1907), pp 87-95.

5. Idem.

6. Ibid., p, 280.

7. Faith of Our Founding Fathers, by Tim LaHaye, Wolgemuth & Hyatt, Publishers, 1987, pp 122-124.

8. Gallard Hunt and James B. Scott, ed., The Debates in the Federal Convention of 1787 Which Framed the Constitution of the United States of America, reported by James Madison (New York: Oxford University Press, 1920), pp. 181-182.

9. William B. Wilcox, ed., The Papers of Benjamin Franklin (New Haven: Yale University Press, 1972) Vol. 15 p. 301.

10. Gaillard Hunt, James Madison and Religious Liberty (Washington: American Historical Association, Government Printing Office, 1902), p. 166.

CHAPTER 8

1. The First Family, Vinyl Album by Cadence Records, 1962.
2. The Awe of God, The Astounding Way a Healthy Fear of God Transforms Your Life, by John Bevere, T. Publishing, an imprint of Thomas Nelson, copyright John T. Bevere, 2023.

CHAPTER 9

1. How Should We Then Live? The Rise and Decline of Western Thought and Culture, by Francis Schaeffer, Fleming H. Revell Co; First Edition, January 1, 1976.

CHAPTER 10

1. How Should We Then Live, by Francis Schaeffer, published by Marshall, Morgan, & Scott, 1976.
2. The 2020 Vote for President by Religious Groups—Christians, by Ryan P. Burge, https://religioninpublic.blog/2021/03/29/the-2020-vote-for-president-by-religious-groups-christians/, January 12, 2023.
3. Percentage of Christian registered voters drops 15% since 2008: Pew, by Jackson Elliott, https://www.christianpost.com/news/percentage-of-christian-voters-drops-15-since-2008-pew.html, November 05, 2020.
4. Political Correctness def., Britannica, by Cynthia Roper, https://www.britannica.com/topic/political-correctness, January 19, 2024.

END NOTES

5. Holy Bible, New International Version®, NIV® Copyright ©1973, 1978, 1984, 2011 by Biblica, Inc.